"The world has come to America and in particular our urban centers. Yet it is hard to find a church that is meeting the need and seizing the opportunity. One that is rising to the challenge is Armitage Baptist Church in Chicago. In my opinion, it is one of the greatest churches in America. Every time I visit Armitage I am blessed and excited by what God is doing. John Thompson's ministry is a key element of the Armitage story. He has lived out urban ministry. A mark of true discipleship is the ability to replicate; John has done so in the lives of numerous Armitage members and in the lives of his own family. His son, Jamie, having grown up under Pastor Lyon's and his father's teachings is growing a church in a tough Chicago location. Read this work, apply its truths, and catch the urban vision. Our nation and the world lie in the balance."

—WILLIAM E. BROWN, PHD

Pastor, North Star Baptist Church and Faculty, Liberty University On-line
Former North American Church Planting professor
Southeastern Baptist Theological Seminary, Wake Forest, NC

"Far from being a beginner text on urban ministry by an inexperienced theorist, *Urban Impact* is written by a pastor who has the experience and credibility that only a lifetime of effective urban work can marshal. Books of this sort sometimes fixate on providing pragmatic ministry Band-aids or become little more than memoirs of social justice written by sympathetic authors living safely outside the city in the comforts of suburbia. In a unique and stirring approach, Thompson deftly crafts his book to become all things to all people. In it, he squares the importance of urban ministry with timeless biblical principles and theological constructs, gives meaty and practical how-tos for those ministering in the urban context, and provides hard statistics that will delight social scientists and academic-types. I predict Thompson's *Urban Impact* will be used in at least two strategic ways: as required reading for students in urban and cross-cultural academic courses, while serving dutifully as a street-smart survival handbook for cross-cultural church planters, city pastors, and para-church workers."

—FREDERICK CARDOZA II, EDD

Department Chair, Christian Ministries,
Associate Professor of Christian Education
Talbot School of Theology and Biola University, La Mirada, CA

"I heartily endorse John Thompson's book, *Urban Impact: Reaching the World through Effective Urban Ministry*. Thompson's work gives a clear theoretical approach to urban ministry, while at the same time offering helpful guidelines on how to do urban ministry. The greatest element about the book is that John knows what he's writing about. John and his family have lived and breathed urban ministry for over a quarter of a century. John's work leaves nothing out for the academician and the practitioner who wish to teach or do urban ministry. This text deals thoroughly with urban ministry elements from the absent father to designing a model to reach the urban environment. Being an academician as well as practitioner, I can appreciate a work that I can personally use in the classroom, as well as in the field."

—LEROY GAINEY, PHD

J. M. Frost Chair of Educational Leadership
Golden Gate Baptist Theological Seminary, Mill Valley, CA, and
Senior Pastor First Baptist Church, Vacaville, CA

"Inner-city ministries may at times be risky and unnerving. But they are never dull, nor without spiritual rewards. John Thompson has given us a book rich in personal narrative, biblical teaching, practical wisdom, and urgent challenge. I recommend that students, who feel even the slightest tug to consider urban ministry, read this book, let its message grip you, and ask God if the inner city is where he wants you to serve him."

—ROGER S. GREENWAY, THD
Professor of World Missiology
Calvin Theological Seminary, Grand Rapids, MI

"John Thompson's book, *Urban Impact*, is like a breath of fresh air amongst the urban ministry literature available today. Thompson addresses the crying need for evangelism and discipleship in the city. He is unafraid to tackle the tough issues, such as pastoral burnout, the negative impact of broken homes, and the challenges of life in urban areas. *Urban Impact* is definitely a "how to" for effective urban discipleship. I heartily recommend *Urban Impact* as a must read for anyone involved in or contemplating ministry in the urban world."

—THOMAS P. JOHNSTON, PHD
Associate Professor of Evangelism
Midwestern Baptist Theological Seminary, Kansas City, MO, and
Pastor, Central Baptist Church, Kansas City, MO

"The Bible speaks a lot about the importance of cities to God, and Jesus wept over the city of Jerusalem. Thompson's work is an important addition to the growing passion people have for urban ministry. Thompson's firsthand experiences give his work a great deal of credibility to an audience who is thirsty to learn all they can about this blossoming field of ministry. In this generation, urban contexts are the most important mission fields of focus, and there are few relevant role models to observe. Thompson's book provides a significant foundation upon which to move into the future for anyone thinking about being part of God's kingdom in an urban context."

—ALLAN KARR, PHD
Missiologist and professor
Golden Gate Baptist Theological Seminary, Mill Valley, CA

"Thompson writes as a pastor, friend, and neighbor of inner-city Chicago. His twenty-nine years living in the city is evident in the personal, practical tone of *Urban Impact.* This is an important contribution to widen our perspective about being missional in the U.S. urban context."

—DAVE LIVERMORE, PHD
Global Learning Center
Grand Rapids Baptist Theological Seminary, Grand Rapids, MI

"There are practitioners who are not veterans. There are veterans who are no longer practitioners. There is nothing like hearing from a veteran who is still a practitioner. John Thompson writes from the field.

"The power of this volume is due in no small part to who John is. I've worked closely with John for a dozen years. I know John's story. It is one of remarkable character and faith. I know John's family. When a family, a minority in its community, lives out robust Christianity with uncommon strength, producing adult children who love God and his work as John's kids do, all the world sits up and takes notice. I know John's community. It is a spiritually, morally, emotionally, hostile environment. It's the last place you would think to find a man choosing to live, serve, and raise a family. I know John's ministry. It is one of unflagging commitment, steady labor, and God-glorifying fruitfulness. He is part of a ministry marked by longevity and impact. He is not theorizing about what could or should happen. He is participating in, observing, and reflecting on what has happened.

"This work helps meet the urgent need for urban ministry perspective and material that is rooted in Scripture, tested in practice, and local-church based. This volume is the voice of a man who lives the life and knows what he is talking about.

"Over half the world is urban, and the rest is quickly being urbanized. We are late and behind in urban missions. We need all the help we can get. This book will educate, equip, and inspire."

—Charles Lyons
Senior Pastor
Armitage Baptist Church, Chicago, IL

"Optimistic. Biblical. Practical. John Thompson's work *Urban Impact: Reaching the World through Effective Urban Ministry* will equip any reader to enter the city with the faith and hope necessary to bring individuals to Jesus Christ. John's book is a long overdue alternative to the whining we hear about urban areas. Today is the day to reach the city, and John's book shows us the way."

—David Mills, PhD
Assistant Dean for Applied Ministries and Assistant Professor of Evangelism
Roy J. Fish School of Missions and Evangelism
Southwestern Baptist Theological Seminary, Fort Worth, TX

"I have read and used many books as texts over the years. *Urban Impact: Reaching the World through Effective Urban Ministry* by John Thompson is the best book I have read on urban ministry, period. I say this for several reasons.

"First, it covers topics that most books on urban ministry do not. In fact, some of the topics I have rarely or never seen addressed in a book on the subject, i.e., urban discipleship and raising a family in the urban environment. His chapters on ministering to the disenfranchised and the impact of the absent father on urban ministry are two of the most important chapters I have read in any book in recent years.

"Second, the book is extremely practical. It not only addresses the problems and the reasons for the problems, but it gives clear step-by-step methods to respond to those problems. This is what students and ministers are looking for. The one comment I consistently receive from my students and the ministers I talk to is that they want materials that are practical. This book is that.

"Third, Thompson writes from years of personal experience. The methods he suggests are valuable because he has utilized them and seen them work. The examples of his personal experiences that are peppered throughout the book bring the methods to life.

"Last, but certainly far from least, the book is biblical. The principles and methods all proceed from Scripture, and Thompson uses Scripture throughout to discuss both the causes of and solutions for problems that are so prevalent in the urban setting. It is vital to me that a book I would use in class or ministry be biblically sound and centered. Thompson's book is both.

"For these reasons, I highly recommend that you consider reading this book. I have known John Thompson for many years. I have had the privilege of seeing him at work in his church in Chicago and of teaching beside him. He is a man of great integrity, knowledge, and experience who has had a positive impact on many people. I am excited because this book will allow that impact to be expanded. The Christian community needs to make use of this book so that more folks can be helped by its truths. I am looking forward to using this book in my classes in the future and to recommending it to colleagues to use as well."

—David R. Penley, PhD
Assistant Professor of Pastoral Counseling
Southwestern Baptist Theological Seminary, Fort Worth, TX

"An illuminating step-by-step guide to establishing an effective urban ministry in today's society."

—Dr. Michael D. Reynolds DMin
Associate Dean, South Chicago Regional Center,
Affiliated Faculty Pastoral Theology-Sociology Department
Trinity International University, Deerfield, IL

"Reading John Thompson's *Urban Impact: Reaching the World through Effective Urban Ministry* was an enlightening experience. John Thompson has captured just what is needed in a comprehensive, yet practical, examination and analysis of and strategy for twenty-first-century urban ministry. Very few other works address the topic so practically while being theologically on target.

"As a professor who for two decades has been teaching a number of courses in this curriculum area, I certainly see this work adopted as a required text in any of three or four courses we offer at our institution. I recommend this work with confidence and enthusiasm."

—Dr. T. Vaughn Walker
WMU Professor of Christian Ministries & Professor of Black Church Studies
The Southern Baptist Theological Seminary, Louisville, KY

"Christian experience and love for and ministry to the city and its people have propelled John Thompson and his whole family into service with love, care, and compassion in the name of the Lord Jesus Christ. His study of the city brings gems that resonate with my spirit. His practical living and approach to many areas of urban ministry bring forth helpful information to train others for further ministry for the twenty-first century. I highly recommend the book *Urban Impact* for those who have a serious call to be an urban minister."

—Robert E. Woolfolk, MA, DHL
Urban Training Center Director
Denver Seminary, Denver, CO

"The urban church and urban ministry have increasingly been the topic of discussion for scholars and practitioners in recent decades. Ray Bakke's book *The Urban Christian* hit a chord and stimulated much of this discussion. Yet there have been few books that have combined good biblical scholarship, sound sociological statements about urbanization, and practical, hands-on guidance on how to be an urban church or do urban ministry. Pastor

John Thompson's *Urban Impact: Reaching the World through Effective Urban Ministry* fills this void.

"Pastor Thompson brings the credentials of twenty-nine years of urban ministry in inner-city Chicago. Furthermore, he represents the lessons learned at Armitage Baptist Church, one of the truly effective and inspiring urban churches in American cities. The lessons he teaches have been tested and found to be true in the daily life of the church and Pastor Thompson and his family.

"One of the many strengths of this book is the emphasis on application. When Pastor Thompson speaks of urban ministry, he provides concrete, well-supported principles that could profitably be followed by any urban church. When he speaks of discipleship, he provides a useful guide as to how to disciple and how to choose the participants for the relationship. His "Living in the City" chapter is wonderful. He speaks with authority about how to raise a family in the city. He speaks of how to engage with the neighborhood. He does this without demonizing the city while at the same time recognizing the challenges and difficulties of living and ministering in the inner city. Lastly, Pastor Thompson provides a wonderful chapter on church planting in urban areas.

"*Urban Impact: Reaching the World through Effective Urban Ministry* is a book that I intend to keep near me on my bookshelf for fast access when I teach courses on urban life and ministry and as I serve in my church in northeastern Minneapolis. In particular, this book would be very useful in academic settings as a text for urban courses and as a very useful guide for the urban ministry practitioner who is looking for a solid biblical approach to urban ministry combined with sociological insights and years of hands-on experience."

—Harley Schreck, PhD
Anthropology and Gerontology
Bethel College, St. Paul, MN

Urban Impact

Urban Impact

Reaching the World through Effective Urban Ministry

John L. Thompson

WIPF & STOCK · Eugene, Oregon

URBAN IMPACT
Reaching the World through Effective Urban Ministry

Wipf & Stock
An Imprint of Wipf and Stock Publishers
199 W. 8th Ave., Suite 3
Eugene, OR 97401
www.wipfandstock.com

ISBN 13: 978-1-60899-658-2

Manufactured in the U.S.A.

I would like to dedicate this book to my faithful Lord who has guided me and helped me in immeasurable ways from conception to conclusion. He is indeed faithful.

Special thanks go to my loving wife Debbie who came to the inner city of Chicago and embraced the challenge of raising our four children in one of the worst neighborhoods in the city, making this our home for the past thirty years.

Contents

Foreword

Some books you read for just one chapter. Such is not the case with John Thompson's wonderful book, *Urban Impact: Reaching the World through Effective Urban Ministry.* If it were the case, I can tell you that the one chapter entitled "The Absent Father: The Greatest Problem in Our Society," would be worth the purchase price of the book and every second of the valuable time that it takes to read it. As very few others have done, John Thompson has not only assessed the problem but provided the reasons for the problem and actually given us a way to address what to many people seems to be an insolvable problem.

Of course, the two chapters on urban discipleship: "Calibrating Our Compass" and "Turn the World Upside Down," along with the two chapters on "Reaching the Disenfranchised" are brimful of cogent information and inspirational challenge. It would be difficult to estimate how important the chapter is on "Living in the City: Achieving Unbounded Success in a Degraded Environment." One reason that chapter is so very important is because for too many evangelical Christians there is a certain attitude of resignation about the possibility of doing anything in the urban areas of America.

Not only does this chapter of John Thompson's book illustrate why that is an erroneous conclusion, but also the very existence of Armitage Baptist Church in Chicago where Thompson serves as Pastor of Discipleship is one of the great untold stories in America today. Beginning with a tiny congregation in an impossible place, Senior Pastor Charles Lyons moved into the community, began to win people to Christ, to live as an example among the people, and then gradually to find a new place to meet when the crowds became so large that he had to look elsewhere. Miraculously, God provided an old Masonic Temple with a perfect location to reach the whole inner city. John Thompson at a later time linked his life with that of Charles Lyons. Charles, the evangelist and preacher, and John, the discipler, have been a great team, and this book grows out of their experiences.

Recently, I had the opportunity to return to the church for a service. I had not been there in several years. The last time I was there, the church was still located in a declining, dilapidated, urban neighborhood even though the church itself had been refurbished and was probably the nicest-looking building in a one-hundred-block radius. But this time when I went back, I noticed something really impressive. The whole neighborhood immediately around the church was coming back. I knew that it was a direct result of the church. While it is true that they have faced the inevitable difficulty of people becoming believers and often moving out of the community, John Thompson has convinced many of the people to stay and plant their lives there in the inner city. As a result, the whole community around them has blossomed unbelievably.

The Armitage Baptist Church just may be the most thoroughly New Testament church in America today. Attending a service there is like attending a meeting of the United Nations. Literally people are from everywhere. Some have PhDs. Others never made it to kindergarten. But they all sit by one another, learn from one another, and bear an incredible witness for Christ.

Although *Urban Impact: Reaching the World through Effective Urban Ministry* is designed primarily to give a handle to those who feel the call of God to the desperate situations in the urban areas of our country, and for that matter the world, it also tells the secret of what God has done at Armitage. If I could only read one book this year on evangelism, and especially how to reach the teeming masses of people in the inner cities of our world, it would be this book by John Thompson. This will change not only your life but also the lives of thousands of others.

Paige Patterson
President, Southwestern Baptist Theological Seminary
Fort Worth, TX

Acknowledgments

Great appreciation goes to Mrs. Dena Owens who tirelessly donated many hours providing editorial assistance. Her labor will always be greatly appreciated.

Also, I owe great thanks to Douglas Knoll for his many hours analyzing my manuscript and giving good advice as well as editorial assistance.

Introduction

"HELP!" IS THE FIRST thought in the mind of one who moves to a large city to minister. What can I do in such a difficult and foreboding environment? Will my family be safe? Where do we start? What do I need to know?

Half of the population of the world lives in cities of one million or more. If we don't reach and disciple people from these masses, our future missionary and pastoral force will be greatly diminished.

This book, *Urban Impact: Reaching the World through Effective Urban Ministry*, is a trumpet call to muster our forces and at the same time deals with the philosophy and practical principles that make any ministry in the city successful. This book is a practical how-to book on growing a successful urban ministry.

In an attempt to be practical, real life experiences are explained to help the reader understand the problems, burdens, and joys of urban ministry, and the powerful impact cities have on the rest of society. How can we leverage this natural influence in order to impact people in the city as well as other parts of our society? Please follow along as we proceed to answer these questions and many others throughout this book.

Unfortunately, there is a tremendous vacuum of pastors and missionaries reaching the masses of people in the cities. This came about because of a great exodus to the suburbs in the 1960s, '70s, and '80s. Christian colleges and seminaries have recognized this need and are mounting a growing emphasis in preparing students to fill the void.

As we discuss the philosophical and biblical foundation for urban ministry, many questions will be answered such as: Why did God design the city? Why is there so much evil? What are the qualities and benefits of cities? What are the problems faced each day by living in large urban areas? How are the cities of our world changing? How is urban ministry both a biblical mandate and the most effective strategy for reaching the world?

The first two chapters of this book, entitled "The Mother of All Challenges" and "A Place of Unparalleled Potential," provide a powerful analysis for addressing the biblical and philosophical need for ministering in urban areas. These chapters also illustrate how planting churches in the city is the most powerful strategy to reach the world. This approach worked for the Apostle Paul and the early church with astounding success, and the power of this strategy is just as effective in the twenty-first century. The church has done a poor job of following this strategy. We can do much better. We must!

The third and fourth chapters of this book discuss biblical principles missing in many ministries. These principles, if practiced, would revolutionize any ministry, but they are strategically necessary in the city. As the seven principles are illustrated, the reader will see their importance as well as their practical necessity.

Chapters 5 and 6 are entitled "Calibrating Our Compass" and "Turn the World Upside Down." One might wonder what two chapters on discipleship are doing in a book on urban ministry. I believe that in twenty-nine years of serving in the city of Chicago, there has been no more effective tool than discipleship to help an urbanite overcome strongholds, become solid spiritually, learn to lead as a good example for others to follow, become a leader, and impact others for Christ. Nowhere in our society is there a greater need for people to come alongside as a mentor; to encourage, hold accountable, and guide another through a destructive and difficult environment. It is my prayer that these chapters will challenge the reader to create a life focus of discipling people, especially those serving in the city.

Chapters 7 and 8 discuss a strategy to reach the disenfranchised. These are the people in the city, especially the inner city, who come from the worst backgrounds and carry the greatest amount of baggage. In these two chapters topics covered are as practical as racial discrimination, dealing with a poor self-image, helping one break addictions of drugs and alcohol, and how to deal with depression, poverty, and homelessness.

Is it really possible to reach people with such debilitating problems? Should I look past them to prospects who don't have as many problems? God has a special love for "the least of these." In a multicultural church with Thirty-seven different nationalities thriving in the inner city of Chicago, we can testify that they can be reached with the gospel, their direction can be reversed, and they can become co-laborers in our mission of discipleship.

A needy follow-up to the chapters on reaching the disenfranchised is the vital chapter 9, "The Absent Father." This chapter covers one of the greatest problems in our society. It is the cause, especially in the city, of most of the societal problems and it has caused the disintegration of the family. This chapter gives helpful advice on how to begin healing the wounds of people who are scarred by this life-debasing component of their childhood and the additional problems that come from a mother who has to fill the gap.

Chapter 10 deals with a topic that is rarely covered in books on urban ministry, "Living in the City." Why are there so few pastors and missionaries moving to the cities? How do we cope with unsafe conditions, the negative environment, and a poor educational system? The chapter is concluded with an exposé about the common problem of burnout in urban ministry and how to prevent and recover from this disorder. Included in Appendix 1 there is a helpful inventory the reader can take to test one's own propensity to burnout.

The final two chapters on planting an urban church are important because the failure of men and women of God who are attempting to plant churches around the world is far too common. These chapters cover seven types of churches one may plant to reach people of multiple ethnicities in the city, and suggest an urban strategy that is being used successfully in numerous urban settings. The valuable section on choosing a team, how to begin, and effective outreach ideas readers will also find to be helpful.

Throughout the book I have shared real life stories for illustration purposes. In order to protect the identity of the subjects in the stories, I have substituted their name with an alias.

Why have we failed so miserably to plant strong churches amidst the masses of people needing the gospel in the cities? The answer to this question may be the greatest hindrance to effective church planting in the cities. This book concludes with a discussion on perhaps the greatest asset to effective church planting in the city. Travel with me through these pages and see if God might tug at your heartstrings and cause you to ask: "Is He calling me to the city?" "If not, how can I pray, support, and send others?"

1

The Mother of All Challenges

Constant Change, Enormous Needs, But-for-God Impossible Difficulties

It was one o'clock in the morning and I awoke with a whining sound in my ears. In the fog of sleep I thought it was the eerie, human-like sound occasionally made by cats as they whine. As the cobwebs began to lift, I could hear the sound of an engine and tires screeching. I soon realized the whining was not a cat at all but the sound of a young lady who was being dragged back and forth in the alley behind my home. As I jumped out of bed and looked out my rear window, I could see someone in the dark hanging out of the passenger side of a car. In the moonlight I could see that the person had little on, with her blouse pulled up over her shoulders and caught in the door mechanism. I screamed for the driver to let the woman go. Slightly afterwards, but almost in tandem, a man in a house across the alley hollered the same words. With a shout, the driver said that he was trying to let her go and as he pushed the door open she fell curled up on the alley pavement. As the car sped away, the woman struggled to her feet. Seeing she was partly naked and in need of help, I asked my wife to take a blouse to her and see if we could bring her into our home or provide help in some way. She took the blouse, refused our help, and began walking down the alley as a blue strobe light began to appear. Such is an example of experiences one may face in the inner city of a large urban area.

Why is there so much evil in the city? What are the qualities and benefits of cities? What are the problems faced each day as one lives in a large urban area? How are the cities of our world changing? How is urban ministry both a biblical mandate and the most effective strategy for reaching people for Jesus Christ? These and other questions will be answered as we explore one of the most amazing and effective opportunities for discipleship known to man.

What do we mean when we use the term urban? The U.S. Government Census Bureau offers a definition of "urbanized areas" as being the fully developed area of a city which may have one or more "central places" and adjacent built-up areas (i.e., suburbs or "urban fringe") with a minimum population of fifty thousand people.[1] "An inner city can be defined as a poverty area in which there is much government activity and control but little activity by the private sector. Often merchandisers, businesses, and churches have left the area. . . . But governmental agencies, public housing, and social institutions are visible."[2]

WHY DID GOD DESIGN THE CITY?

According to Redeemer Magazine, God designed the city to be first of all "a place of refuge and shelter for the weak. . . . The earliest cities provided refuge from wild animals and marauding tribes and criminals. . . . In Israel, God designated certain cities to be 'cities of refuge'. . . . Today the city is a place where minorities can cluster for support in an alien land, where new immigrants can work together for a foothold in a new world, where refugees can find shelter, and where the homeless and poor can better eke out an existence."[3] The weak and powerless need the city because they cannot survive in the suburbs and small towns.

Secondly, God designed the city "as a cultural and human development center. The city stimulates and forces the gifts, capacities, and talents of people, the deep potentialities in the human heart." To summarize the Redeemer Magazine article: The city brings you into contact with so many people with different abilities and skills, producing greater works of art, science, technology, and culture. Even the description of the new Babylon shows the power of the city to develop culture. In Revelation 18 we see the city is a place of music and the arts (v. 22a), of crafts and manufacturing (v. 22b), of technological advance (v. 23a), and of trade and retailing (v. 23c).[4]

1. U.S. Census Bureau. *Classification*, 2000.
2. Marciniak, *Reviving*, lecture.
3. Redeemer, *City*, 2.
4. Ibid.

Thirdly, God designed the city "as a place of spiritual searching and temple building. Ancient cities were built around a "ziggurat"—the original skyscrapers—temples where a particular god was thought to "come down." Cities were the royal residences of the god, and the city was dedicated to him or her. When God creates a new city in the desert, he does so by dwelling among his people in the tabernacle, for the city of God will be his dwelling place. Later, in the earthly city of Jerusalem, the city stands as the central integrating point of the city's architecture and as apex of its art and science and technology. Thus *any* city has a spiritual vacuum within it. The turmoil and climate of cities make people religious seekers. Protestant Christians abandoning the city inevitably make it easier for the city to turn to false gods.[5]

A COMMUNITY OF ASSETS AND LIABILITIES

As millions of immigrants approached the coast of the United States at New York City, they were met by the Statue of Liberty with an inscription printed on the base of the monument with these words: "Give me your tired, your poor, your huddled masses yearning to be free. . . . Send these, the homeless, tempest-tossed to me." Since the earliest settlers traveled from England to this country, America has been a country of immigrants. During the nineteenth century, huge numbers met the Statue of Liberty as they came in waves to escape poverty, famine, political unrest, or persecution. Many came for better education or for personal advancement. On every continent, large cities are the gateways to the world, the port of entry for millions of immigrants. Ray Bakke states, "The twentieth century has produced the greatest global migration in the history of the world. The Southern hemisphere is coming North; East is coming West and everyone is coming to the cities."[6]

Cities are known for diversity. The ethnicity of the world is clearly present in the cities. Ray Bakke has stated, "Yesterday, cities were in the nations; today all the nations are in the cities."[7] More immigrants entered the United States in the 1990s than in any previous decade.[8] The largest immigrant populations are in New York, Los Angeles, and Chicago, respectively.[9]

5. Ibid.
6. Bakke, *Theology*, 116.
7. Ibid., 117.
8. Singer, *Immigrant Gateways*, 5.
9. Ibid.

Immigrant Gateways, Year 2001[10]		
City	Foreign-Born Population	Percent Foreign-Born
New York	2,871,032	35.9
Los Angeles	1,512,720	40.9
Chicago	628,903	21.7
Houston	516,105	26.4
San Jose	329,757	36.8
San Diego	314,227	25.7
Dallas	290,436	24.4
San Francisco	285,541	36.8
Phoenix	257,325	19.5
Miami	215,739	59.5

This immigrant growth will not end anytime soon. According to environmental writer Mark Nowak, it is estimated that "60 percent of the population increase in the United States between 1994 and 2050 will be attributed to immigration and the descendents of immigrants."[11]

Cities are known for their assets. Cities are abundant with many cultural, recreational, entertainment, and educational institutions. Opportunities to learn through their many colleges, seminars, and conferences are abundant. The range of merchandise is enormous, making it possible to purchase almost anything conceivable. Though large cities are diverse in what they offer, cities are also known for specialization. For example, New York is known as the financial center of the world. Until the more modern era, Los Angeles was known as the entertainment capital of the world, and, not too long ago, Chicago was known as a manufacturing city. Therefore, large cities are abundant in resources that can truly enhance the daily lives of their citizens.

Cities are known for their problems. I agree with Charles Lyons, Senior Pastor at Armitage Baptist Church in Chicago, when he says,

10. Singer, *Metro. Geography*, 7.

11. Nowak, *Immigration*, 2.

"In the city everything is intensified, magnified, and multiplied." With tongue in cheek he goes on to say, "Ministering in the city is like tent camping in a hurricane." This tempest-filled environment is expressed on a daily basis in many ways:

The problem of stress: Those who live in large urban areas experience extra stress in day-to-day living. In the larger cities rush hour traffic has expanded to most of the day, traffic tickets have become a major form of government revenue, there are long lines at government agencies like the Post Office and the Department of Motor Vehicles, and you have to wade through the bureaucracy when dealing with issues such as traffic tickets, property taxes issues, errors in utility bills, city service problems, and accident reports, to name a few.

Several years ago the county made a mistake on my property tax bill, charging me double what they should have based on the assessed value. Since my bank was automatically paying my taxes through escrow withholdings, the big jump in my tax bill was paid without the bank noting the increase. I soon received a notice that my house payment would increase by about fifty dollars per month for two years because of an increase in property taxes. Because I was an inner-city missionary at the time, and living on minimal income, I could not afford this increase, so I quickly went downtown to the county tax department and endured a frustrating meeting before finally convincing the clerk that there was, in fact, an error made on my bill. He proceeded to fill out a Declaration of Error assuring me that I would receive a $1,000.00 refund. Even though the error was obvious, the tax complaint would have to go through the Court of Appeals, which was a two-year process. I did get the refund without, of course, the benefit of interest and only after my family lived through a very stressed budget for the two-year waiting period. During my twenty-nine year tenure in Chicago, I have also gone through time consuming and frustrating experiences trying to correct a major error with the water department as well as with the county property tax bill.

High cost of living: In Chicago, apartment rentals run from $500 to $5,000 per month. In the neighborhood near our church, assuming you stay off the boulevard, the rent will be between $800 and $1,800 per month. The ten most overpriced places to live in 2004 were all cities with a population of 240,055 or more. Among the cities included, Seattle ranked as number one, Chicago as number eight, and New York City ranked as number nine. Below I have included these ten most overpriced places from an article by Betsy Schiffman, published in Forbes Magazine.[12]

Ten Most Overpriced Places in 2004					
City	Job Growth Rank	Income Growth Rank	Cost Of Living	Housing Afford-ability	Median Home Price
Seattle, WA	122	149	132	122	$282,500
Bergen-Passaic, NJ	110	102	141	131	$379,400
Miami, FL	79	132	127	137	$254,900
Portland, OR	118	133	114	105	$195,100
Middle-sex, NJ	85	131	138	116	$322,700
San Jose, CA	150	28	149	142	$585,000
San-Francisco, CA	145	27	150	146	$597,300
Chicago, IL	119	98	123	120	$228,100
New York, NY	103	63	146	143	$369,700
Jersey City, NJ	98	101	119	135	N/A

According to the article, the rankings in Forbes' Best Places To Do Business are based on a 1 to 150 scale, where 1 is the best and 150 is

12. Schiffman, Forbes Mag., *Overpriced.*

> *the worst. A city that ranks 150 for its cost of living, for example, is the absolute worst of all 150 places in the list. (The rankings used in this list were based on data from Economy.com and Sperling's Best Places). The median home prices were taken from the National Association of Realtors' fourth-quarter report on existing family home sales, where the national average was $170,800. (The median home price in Jersey City was not available, however, and the median home price in San Jose came from the Santa Clara County Association of Realtors). The cities are ranked in the order of the most overpriced to the least overpriced.*

Deteriorated neighborhoods: As David Claerbaut states,

> If the demand for housing decreases in the neighborhood, trouble insures. Since the housing supply is fixed, this dip will drop prices, which will alarm financial institutions and cause them to cut back on loans. This cutback is called redlining. Redlining begins with bank officials outlining an area that they feel will decline over the next twenty years (the length of many mortgages). As a result of this prediction, the bank chooses not to lend any mortgage money to anyone wishing to purchase land in the redlining area. Though illegal, this practice is used to protect the bank against high-risk lending. What is happening, however, is that the bank, ostensibly a servant of the community, becomes its killer. The result of these redlining practices was that portions of the inner city took on the appearance of a ghost town as the area becomes dotted with burned out, abandoned buildings, surrounded by open space.[13]

Another related problem is the depressing conditions due to the deteriorating property owned by slum landlords who have little concern for their tenants. Some homes in the inner city are not only unpleasant but also unsafe due to structural problems and rat infestations.

Urban renewal: Another common occurrence in urban properties is gentrification, which leads to urban renewal. I agree with David Claerbaut when he said,

> There is always the ever-present fear of urban redevelopment (once called urban renewal) in its various forms, even where housing is adequate. Urban renewal was sardonically viewed as a euphemism for poor-people removal. Redevelopment is no different. What occurs is that a city marks off an area (much the

13. Claerbaut, *Urban*, 40–41.

> way a bank redlines) and decides to refurbish the neighborhood. However, this refurbishing does not benefit the present inhabitants of the community, as many people believe; rather, the area is 'cleaned out,' meaning that the existing buildings are leveled and new construction occurs."[14] Sometimes these redevelopment programs have been termed land reclamation. This is a most interesting term. When broken down, it simply states that the land is being reclaimed.[15]

The renewal only helps the property owners, raising the value of property and causing the tax and insurance to also go up, thus forcing rent skyward. The unfortunate result is that the poor people are forced out of their homes to even worse neighborhoods. This is happening in a major way in the neighborhood where I live. The environment is improving because drug traffic and gang activity is decreasing: but because of higher rent, the poor people are forced to move to worse living conditions.

Housing projects: Many of the very poor are forced to live in a system of housing projects, which has become a failed sociological experiment. In the book *A Heart for City*, David Brown and Dana Thomas in their chapter titled "Ministering in the Projects" maintain, "Today the Chicago Housing Authority operates approximately 40,000 homes and apartments."[16] These units are often poorly maintained. Imagine coming home with your groceries to walk up fifteen flights to your apartment because the elevators don't work. This is often the experience of residents who live in urban housing projects.

Single parent homes: Households with one parent are very common in urban areas, especially in the inner city. Other than the absence of a relationship with Jesus Christ as Savior, I know of no factor that more clearly and completely impairs a person's life in so many ways than the absence of a father. We visited one home with five children all fathered by different men, none of whom lived with them. The grandmother living in the same home was also sleeping with a boyfriend who was not her husband. In the city, especially the inner city, there are few examples of good male role models and few examples of good marriages, making it hard to develop male leadership.

14. Ibid., 118.
15. Ibid., 119.
16. Brown and Thomas, *Heart for City*, 391.

Corruption in government: In large cities there is a problem with corruption in government and the police force. Police are often rude and uncivil to youth, especially minorities, stopping and frisking them with no probable cause. My two sons and my son-in-law have been frisked many times. On one occasion they were searched while waiting for a Christian youth organization's doors to be opened so they could attend the youth program. These negative experiences make it hard to teach youth to respect civic authorities.

Gang activity: There is much gang activity in large cities, especially in the inner city. Humboldt Park, one half mile south of Armitage Baptist Church, has been designated by a gang expert at the University of Chicago as being the worst gang neighborhood in the country. "In the metropolitan Chicago area, an estimated 100,000 young people are involved in gangs. The largest is the Latin Disciples, with about 10,000 members. . . . There are about 120 different gangs in the Chicago area."[17] In many neighborhoods in Chicago, residents often hear gunfire outside their homes, which is usually gang-related.

Illegal drugs: Street gangs are often actively engaged in selling drugs throughout the city. Most metropolitan areas, especially in the United States, have a huge illegal drug trade. Billions of dollars are spent each year to lessen the drug traffic through legal action and education, but even more money than this is made on the street selling these drugs. In Chicago, it is possible for young kids ("shortys"), only ten to sixteen years old, to make $800 to $1,000 a week for being a lookout ("spotter") for drug dealers. It is no surprise in a community where the unemployment rate is over 50 percent that some would seek this type of income. In the inner city, drug trafficking is not conducted with a high level of secrecy. Residents often see drug exchanges take place right outside their homes. By using "spotters" and by moving their pickup location every thirty minutes or so, it becomes more challenging for the police to make arrests.

Poor public education: Cities often have poor public education with a dropout rate at some high schools as high as 75 percent. David Claerbaut suggests five of the reasons for this lack of educational achievement: 1. "The role models of the poor are from the ranks of the unemployed, unskilled, alcoholic, disabled, and criminal. Ironically, the criminal group includes the most affluent of the lot: the three Ps—prostitutes, pimps, and pushers." 2. "Limited formal education of the parent(s), coupled with the

17. Locke, *Heart for City*, 437.

lack of opportunity in general, so that the youth usually has little contact with books."[18] These children often don't have the luxury of parents reading to them when they are small to create a hunger and interest in reading. 3. "Bulging classes, filled to the brim with academically needy youngsters, are the rule rather than the exception." 4. "The condition of the schools and academic materials."[19] Buildings are old and expensive to maintain, therefore, the money is eaten up in maintenance and the large bureaucracy. 5. "Poor education is the result of teacher transience and lack of accountability."[20] Experienced teachers leave the inner-city school for better teaching conditions, leaving the inner-city schools with a high percentage of first-year teachers.

Homelessness: There is a major homeless problem in every large city. It is estimated that there are between two and three million homeless people in the United States, mostly in large cities.[21] According to the U.S. government, estimates are that 200,000 homeless people are mentally ill, which equals one third of the homeless population.[22] Some have fallen on hard times, but many simply do not want to live in shelters. They feel they are losing their independence.

How do problems in the city impact the church, which is seeking to survive and grow in this hostile environment?

First, there are many transitional communities in large cities. The neighborhood where I have lived for the past twenty-six years was once Jewish, then it changed to Swedish/Danish, then Puerto Rican, and now it is Puerto Rican/African American with a large increase in young urban professional (Yuppie) residents. This is a tremendous struggle for the local church to minister in an ever-changing environment with changing cultures, especially when the new culture also has a different language. These new residents don't feel comfortable in a church that expects them to assimilate into their type of worship and style of ministry.

Second, people in the city are transitory. Many are apartment dwellers, often moving from apartment to apartment. Being fluid, they often move out of a church's area, causing the church to lose people, which of-

18. Claerbaut, *Urban*, 99.

19. Ibid., 100.

20. Ibid.

21. Greenway and Monsma, *Cities*, 183.

22. Adair, *Lighthouse*, 105.

ten include leaders and teachers. Because of this transitory nature, they need the church and its staff to be a picture of stability.

Third, there are unique problems associated with growth in the large cities. It has been said, "If you don't grow, you die." "Where there is no vision the people perish" (Prov 29:18 KJV). I had a seminary professor who used to say, "It's growth or the grave, expand or expire." In the city, however, it can be said, *if you grow you die*. Church growth brings its own set of problems:

- In the inner city, church income is low with a lower percentage of income-producing breadwinners.
- Buildings in most cities are from ninety to 110 years old. That means not only do the homeowners have greater upkeep and remodeling expenses but also that the church, which usually occupies old buildings, has these expenses as well.
- There are high remodeling expenses with skilled union labor charging approximately fifty dollars or more per hour.
- Because of the mass migration to the suburbs by the middle class, the city has lost many of its tradesmen, teachers, and leaders. These are people with the skills that are desperately needed by a growing church.
- Because of the mass migration referred to above the city church usually has a leadership vacuum, putting more pressure and need with the few leaders it has, dwarfing the potential for quality.
- In the urban church there is a high ratio of parishioners to staff. Because of the extra burden and larger concentration of people, the urban church needs more staff than the average non-city church. The main reason the urban church has a lower staff number is because of a lower rate of giving by its people and thus a lower church income, forcing the church to hire fewer staff than churches of the same size in the suburbs. This dilemma raises the rate of burnout by people serving in an urban environment. According to a survey of 1,200 women (those who attended the 1994 national convention of the Christian Community Development Association, and also women outside the organization engaged in urban ministry) on the greatest challenges or frustrations in urban ministry, 70 percent rated burnout as the most difficult to cope with, rating it

from moderate to very significant.[23] At Armitage Baptist Church, we have nearly 1,000 people attending our morning worship with only about 550 of them who are members. By the time people who are attending college and people who are not really committed are subtracted, about 350 volunteers carry the burden for the total 1,000.

- Most urban churches do not have the luxury of parking facilities. Where do you park your attendees when the church is situated in a residential community and you have one parking lot (if any) that will handle twenty cars? Local residents don't go to work and free up parking space on Sunday morning, they sleep in. At Armitage, we are fortunate to have purchased one parking lot that holds 50 cars. We were also able to get permission from our local police district to park cars on the restricted boulevard Sunday mornings, and we borrow parking from the local bank. We also rent a nearby grade school parking lot about three blocks away from the church, shuttling people by van from our remote parking to our building every Sunday morning. A team of parking attendants work outside, communicating with two-way radios about available parking spots.
- If a building is purchased in the city, it will undoubtedly need rehabilitation. Who will do the work if you can't afford to hire contractors?
- Apartment dwellers know little about remodeling a building, and it will be difficult to hire it done with the typical low urban church income. At Armitage, we have had to bring in scores of construction teams from sister churches throughout the nation to assist us on our rehab projects.
- If an urban church is growing, it is going to run out of space. The cost of property is high in the city. In our area, a house, which would be two or three flats (two or three floors with a family living on each floor), runs between $200,000 and $500,000 each. These houses are sitting on a twenty-five or thirty-five-foot-wide parcel of land that runs about one hundred feet deep. To acquire enough land to build on, you would have to purchase three or

23. Garriott, *Progeny*, 25.

> more houses next to each other and tear them down. Before you begin to build, you would have accumulated at least one and a half million dollars in preparatory expenses.

As you can see, problems in the city are great. Each of these problems directly impedes the urban church's ability to grow. But we have an awesome God who can solve each and every problem; as God stated to Abraham with the question, "Is anything too difficult for the LORD?" (Gen 18:14).

REVIEW QUESTIONS

1. Define the term "urbanized area."
2. Define the term "inner city."
3. What are three reasons God designed the city?
4. Explain the three qualities that are unique to large cities.
5. What are three problems in the city impacting a church that is seeking to survive and grow?

2

A Place of **Unparalleled** Potential

A Biblical Prescription for Worldwide Impact

FOR THE PAST HUNDRED or so years there has been a massive shift in the population of people groups all over our world. According to the United Nations, in 1900 over 13 percent of the world's population was urban. By the year 2005, the number grew to about 49 percent, with more-developed nations at about 76 percent urban.[1] In 2010, according to the United Nations, 3.49 billion people lived in urban areas. That means as of 2010, 51 percent of the world population is now urban.[2] Therefore, as of July 2007, for the first time in history, over half of the world's population became urban. According to current trends, it is estimated that by the year 2030, 61 percent of the population of the world will reside in the cities.[3] In 1900 there were only twelve cities in the world with a population of one million, or more, people. As of 2000, there were 411 cities in the world of more than one million people and forty-one "megacities," defined as cities of five million people or more. In 1950 there was only one city that had more then ten million inhabitants. By 2015, twenty-three cities are projected to hold over ten million people; all but four will be less developed countries.[4] Ray Bakke wrote that "we will add one billion people to the planet in the next ten years, mostly in Asia and primarily in the cities."[5] What is the influence or power that has caused such a surge in migration to the cities of our world? Without

1. World Urbanization Prospectus, 2005.
2. World Population, *Growth*, 2009, 91.
3. World Population Division, 2003.
4. World Urbanization Prospectus, 1999, 8.
5. Bakke, *Theology*, 13.

question there are sociological and political reasons for this migration, but the real power behind this massive movement is our sovereign God. In Psalm 24:1 it says, "The earth is the LORD's, and all it contains." God is the sovereign master and owner of the universe. He is not an absentee God but is actively directing the affairs of mankind. There is one power behind this massive movement of humanity. God is strategically moving the masses of mankind for a fundamental purpose. Most conservative Bible scholars agree that the coming of our Lord is imminent. We believe that the clock is winding down and that we are in the last years before the return of our Lord. God is passionately seeking those who would follow him and has commanded us to disciple people from all over the world. Because of the shortness of time, I believe God is flooding people all over the world to our doorsteps so it will be easier for us to reach them.

This is not only a foreign phenomenon. As of 1990, more than 50 percent of all Americans lived in thirty-nine metro areas of more than one million.[6] According to Wikipedia, 81 percent of the population of North America resided in cities and suburban areas as of mid-2005 (the worldwide urban rate was 49 percent).[7] God is urbanizing his world. Roger Greenway says, "At no time in history has it been more true than now that he who wins the city, wins the world."[8]

God's interest in cities is not only a twentieth and twenty-first century certainty. The city is not just a sociological phenomenon or invention of mankind. The city is God's invention and design. God's plan for our eternal dwelling place is in a city (Rev 21). Even Abraham recognized that, and it is said, "He was looking for the city which has foundations, whose architect and builder is God" (Heb 11:10).

According to Ray Bakke, "The word city or cities occurs some 1,250 times in the Bible. There are 140 cities listed in the Scriptures. Sodom is mentioned fifty-one times."[9] When God wanted to reach the Assyrians, he did not just send his prophet to an Assyrian country but sent Jonah to the great city of Nineveh. Jesus had compassion for the city. As he was approaching his triumphal entry into Jerusalem, coming over the hill and seeing the city, he wept (Luke 19:41). His weeping was for the great masses of people who had rejected him.

6. Ibid., 157.

7. Wikipeda, 2010.

8. Greenway, *Apostles to City*, 11.

9. Bakke, *Heart for City*, 19.

GOD'S MOST EFFECTIVE STRATEGY

Traditionally, missions were referred to as the hinterlands, the rural areas of the world. With the advent of the Industrial Revolution people began moving to the cities. But while the world has been changing in dramatic ways, missionary agencies have only begun to prioritize reaching urban areas in the past few decades. While the world's population has been migrating to the cities, missionaries have continued to gravitate to the small towns, especially with church-planting efforts in the United States. This change in priority is slow, partially because the sending church still conceives "real missionary work" as work in the tribal areas. Fortunately, this view is changing. Ray Bakke stated it well when he said, "Missions is no longer about crossing the oceans, jungles, and deserts, but about crossing the streets of the world's cities."[10]

Much can be gained by studying the missionary work described in the New Testament. The greatest example can be found in the life of the Apostle Paul who was well prepared for his mission. Born and raised in the Gentile city of Tarsus, Paul was a Roman citizen. He understood the Greek culture, Roman law, Gentile society, and pagan religions; he therefore knew profoundly the people to whom he had been called to minister.[11]

Most of the theology that we have came from the Pauline Epistles. It is time that we begin patterning our mission strategy after the strategy that Paul followed. As he planned his mission trips, Paul simply plotted the larger cities and moved from one to the next, planting churches everywhere he went.

The entire ministry of the Apostle Paul was focused on cities. He spent most of his second missionary journey in Corinth, the largest city in Greece with 600,000 people. In his third missionary journey, Paul spent three years in Ephesus, the largest city in Asia Minor. Paul went from city to city and spent most of his time in the largest metropolitan areas. Apparently his strategy worked. Research shows that nearly two-thirds of the population of the Roman Empire were Christians and were established in major urban areas.[12]

10. Bakke, *Theology*, 13.
11. Linthicum, *Urban Churches*, 167.
12. Stark, *Cities of God*, 6, 13–14, 60.

Why would an all-wise God choose the city as the most effective place for missionary work? Cities are best suited for missionary work for several reasons. First, Christianity spreads better in the city because of the personal openness of urban people. People are more open to the gospel in the city because of the rapid change that is a part of urban life and the personal turmoil that is part of the urban experience. Therefore, evangelism, humanly speaking, is easier in the city. Second, cities are best suited for missionary work because of cultural influences. The city is the place where culture is formed. It is the seat of power for the media, education, academia, the arts, and literature. Thus, as the city goes, so goes the nation. The third reason cities are so well suited for missionary work is because of global connection. The city is the place where many nationalities and ethnic groups come together. The spread of the gospel in the city automatically moves Christianity into many ethnic people groups and thus into dozens and scores of countries. The fourth reason that cities are so well suited for missionary work has been taught by Missiologists for many years: Immigrants experience their greatest period of responsiveness to the gospel in the first five years of their migration. They are more responsive because they have often broken ties with their friends, family, and religion in order to come to their new country.

Charles Lyons, Senior Pastor at Armitage Baptist Church, describes the city as a center of influence. My synopsis of his description is as follows: He begins by describing the city as a giant hilltop. As it rains, the water flows down the hill by finding natural channels flowing to the valley below. Upon these hilltops, it rains down all the good, bad, and ugly. For example, small towns don't have the Field Museum of Natural History, the New York Opera, or the Boston Red Socks. Small towns just can't develop and maintain the great cultural and entertainment establishments found in every large city. Where did breakdancing come from? Where did rap music, blues, or hip hop come from? They all came from the large cities. Now, in a cornfield in Iowa, little boys can be seen with their jeans hanging down to their knees. If someone in that small town invented a new type of music, it would never get off the ground because the mechanisms—the studios, promoters, and publishers—found in the cities are needed to distribute it.

Satan also uses the natural channels that influence society to do his evil works, and the most effective place for Satan to work is through the channels found in cities. The city provides fertile soil for Satan's evil tactics because it contains masses of people compounded by the great exodus of the 1960s, '70s, and '80s when the salt and light left the cities in mass numbers. (This will be explored in more detail later in this chapter). Satan has a fertile field to accomplish his work through the natural channels of the city so he can influence the rest of society.

Where did AIDS expand and spread? It was the cities where it multiplied. It is in the cities where the largest concentrations of gay people reside, and it is also where the largest amount of drug use and dirty needles can be found, spreading the disease. Where did pornography come from? It was manufactured and distributed in the cities. Forty or fifty years ago it was difficult for most people to get pornography. If they found a source dealing in this contraband, the clerk would go to the back room and discretely bring the pornography out to the buyer. Now it is available in retail establishments in every small town in this country, right out in the open for all to see. In Chicago, where Playboy Enterprises originated, there is even a street named after its founder: Hugh Hefner Drive.

Where did gangs originate? Now small towns all over this nation are complaining about gang problems. Where did illegal drugs originate? When I was a teenager in my medium-sized town, you heard very little about drugs. The drug of choice for my classmates was alcohol. But in the large cities, all types of drugs were imported, packaged, and distributed. Today in most small towns, it is easy to purchase just about whatever drug desired.

Cities are hilltops of cultural influence, hilltops of political influence, hilltops of satanic influence, and are also hilltops of spiritual influence. As it rains down on the hilltops, the large cities of our world, influence flows down the natural channels to the rest of society. People continually move from the city to the suburbs thinking they can flee the problems of the city. It's only a matter of time before the influence of the city—the good, bad, and ugly—invade the peaceful environment of small-town America.

Satan is not the only life-changing influence that can flow from those hilltops to the rest of society. The influence of God can best impact society if it is maximized on these hilltops. In the book of Acts, Luke tells us of Paul's work in Ephesus. According to this passage, Paul began teaching at the school of Tyrannus, which was held at a small outdoor amphitheater where Paul taught daily. Luke said, "This took place for two years, so that all who lived in Asia heard the word of the Lord, both Jews and Greeks" (Acts 19:10). All who lived in Asia heard the gospel, Jews as well as Greeks. What an incredible impact Paul had as the Word of the Lord flowed down the hilltop of Ephesus to all of Asia. Dwight L. Moody said, "Waters run downhill and the highest hills in America are the great cities. If we can stir them we shall stir the whole country."[13]

Why are there so many problems in the city? Why is the city so evil? Early in the history of the world the city became a refuge from God. When God drove Cain from the land, he built a city as a refuge from God (Gen 4:17). Large cities provide an ideal refuge for people to flee to. People with divergent lifestyles can run and hide because a city is a dynamic environment where the weak and different are tolerated. The criminal, the sexual deviant, those who practice alternate lifestyles that are not accepted by society at large, people who choose to not work in the traditional sense but find their livelihood by panhandling, some who are living in cardboard boxes under freeway overpasses, as well as many others who are looking for a place of refuge.

The city provides a culture that seeks to defy God. The city of Babel, for example, was built for human glory instead of God's glory. In Genesis 11:4, it records that the people of Babel said, "Come, let us build for ourselves a city, and a tower whose top will reach into heaven, and let us make for ourselves a name, otherwise we will be scattered abroad over the face of the whole earth." The city is a place where we can use human resources to make a name for ourselves. This kind of attitude leads to idolatry of achievement. As a cultural production center, the city is like a magnifying glass, bringing out whatever is in the human heart. Thus, the city brings out the best and at the same time the very worst of human nature.

The city is also a place of idolatry, as we see with the city of Babylon. Today people are drawn to skyscraper temples, worshipping self and money. There is more wealth per capita in large cities than any other place on earth, man worshiping money and self. Cities are also a hotbed of religious cults and false teaching. Since cities breed spiritual seekers, when Christians abandon the cities, the seekers fall into the hands of these false teachers, idols, and heresies.

If you add to these natural tendencies the lack of Christian influence per capita in the late twentieth and twenty-first centuries, there is

13. Hudson, *Churches*, 141.

no wonder that the decline of morality, along with the massive amount of sin-related problems, has increased significantly.

In the 1960s, '70s, and '80s, Christians fled the city in massive numbers along with many from the middle class who were flooding the suburbs. There were many reasons for their exodus. Some claim racial discrimination as the motivator. There may have been some racial prejudice as a reason, but the cities have always been filled with ethnic diversity. The primary reason these people left was to seek a better life, the "American dream." They were looking for better education for their children, a safer living environment free from gang activity, drugs, and violence. In many urban centers there was a mass exodus of jobs; many of the factories moved because business manager were also looking to escape the higher cost of operating in the city. Many companies have even left our country looking for cheap labor. In Chicago, as in other places, the white people left first, followed by middle class African Americans, with the middle class Hispanic population close behind. Today there are large numbers of minority people of almost every kind living in the suburbs around large cities.

The primary reason so many believers left with the rest of the middle class was so they, too, could chase the American dream. What happens when we lose the preservative? We are left with rot and deterioration. The salt and light left the city and we are left with the effects. I am convinced that if the body of Christ had seen the Great Commission as an important part of their purpose for existence—if they had stayed in order to respond to a greater purpose—our cities as well as our country would not be as morally bankrupt as it is today. One would think that the command Jesus made in Matthew 6:33 was to seek first the American dream, and its benefits and the kingdom of God will be added to you. "The kingdom of God and his righteousness" is what we are to seek. If we do that, God promises to provide all of our needs (v. 31, 33), and there will be no need to worry (v. 34). The worries of this world are what the Gentiles sought (v. 32) but, unfortunately, in our age this became the idol of many believers as well. We are not called to comfort and prosperity. We are called to a mission, and the mission is better achieved where the masses live. God is urbanizing the world, bringing the world to our doorsteps so we can reach them.

Where are all the people from? They are from every nation and ethnic group in the world. Only a mile northwest of my church in

Chicago is a large Polish community. In fact, Chicago has one of the largest Polish populations in the world with over 280,000 (840,000 in the greater metropolitan area) people from their mother country, second only to Warsaw, Poland. Far more Jewish people live in New York City than in the whole state of Israel. In the greater Chicago area there are 300,000 people of Jewish descent along with 400,000 Muslims. The Chicagoland area draws 1.5 million Hispanics who come from many Latin American countries, the greatest percentages coming from Mexico and Puerto Rico. Chinese people live en masse in every major city in the United States. As Bakke asks, "How is it that 80 million Chinese now live outside of China? The Christian church has been struggling to get the gospel into China since the Nestorians traveled the Silk Road in the seventh century."[14] Now God is putting them in every city in the world. We have about sixty-six nations represented in our city, which is typical of every large city in this America. The world has indeed come to our front door.

Imagine hundreds of thousands of people from every nation of the world moving into your neighborhood. The world lands at our doorstep and Christians flee from the cities in droves, chasing the American dream.

Why aren't more pastors and church planters going to the cities? If 50 percent of the world lives in the cities, shouldn't 50 percent of pastors and missionaries go to the cities? The fact is that we need many more than half of the new pastors and missionaries because of the mass exodus talked about earlier. Unfortunately, we are not seeing large numbers of men moving into the large cities of the world. The search for pleasure and the world's values has even invaded the pulpits and the seminaries of our country.

We have found it very difficult to recruit pastors and church planters who are willing to move to Chicago. "It's too dangerous there!" When I moved to Chicago twenty-nine years ago, I was warned by many friends that I should not take my young family to the inner city of Chicago. It was too dangerous, and the environment was not suited for raising children. In those days God gave me a response that I have lived by ever since. "The safest place in all the world is in the center of God's will, and the dangerous place is out of his will." After twenty-nine years I can say that God has been faithful. He has protected my family and the evils of

14. Bakke, *Urban World*, 75, 76.

the city have not destroyed or even diminished the growth and spiritual development of my children. My children are adults now and each one is a committed believer in Jesus Christ, all serving the Lord with their spouses in the city. They have gained an appreciation and love for people of many cultures and understand our mission to reach the masses.

I firmly believe that the worst place to raise your children is in a Christian home where humanism rules and where self and materialism are gods. If you have a home where Christ rules, your children will be okay. Yes, the cost of living is greater in the city and the income for people in ministry is less, but it is time that we put feet to our theology. Is our belief in a good and sovereign God, a God who insures that all things truly do "work together for good to those who love God, to those who are called according to his purpose" (Rom 8:28)? Is this a belief we live by or is it just something we teach others? Yes, there are many frustrations and inconveniences in the city. Yes, there is stress and discouragement, but "God is able to make all grace abound to you, so that always having all sufficiency in everything, you may have an abundance for every good deed" (2 Cor 9:8).

As pastors and missionaries look for places to serve, we should consider where the greatest need is and where we can have the greatest impact for the kingdom of God. In Valdosta, Georgia, there is a Southern Baptist church for every 1,800 people. In Denver, Colorado, there is a Baptist church for every 59,000 people. In Dallas, Texas, it seems that there is a Baptist church on every corner. Where are the guys who are being called to the tough places, to the inner cities of our world? I am convinced that it is not a matter of God not calling them; it is more a matter of his servants not listening.

CONCLUSION

What was God's plan to reach the world? In order to win people to Christ and plant churches, Paul didn't go to a haystack in the countryside. Paul went to the cities, one after another. Paul wrote his Epistles to the churches he had planted in the cities and to the people he had discipled. The New Testament plan was to plant Truth Centers on hilltops (the cities) and allow the truth of God's Word to flow to the rest of society.

A major missions leader in one of our most prestigious seminaries once told me, "If we don't follow an ambitious, concerted effort to reach our cities in America, our missions movement will go down the tube." If half of the people live in the cities of one million or more, then half of our missionaries and church planters must be developed and recruited from these cities. If they aren't, our missions force will be severely depleted as we are seeing in many fields like that of Mexico City where many of our missionaries are at retirement age with no replacement.

From the hilltops of our world flow all the cultural trends and influences of society. If we can plant thriving New Testament churches in the cities, all of society will be impacted. People abound in cities. It is through the cities that we can impact the world. God is bringing the world to our doorsteps, and we must cooperate with God's plan while there is still time.

REVIEW QUESTIONS

1. How is the shifting population an enormous tool God is using to build his kingdom?
2. What was the strategy that the Apostle Paul followed in his extraordinary missionary endeavor?
3. What are four reasons, cited by the author, that cities are dynamically suited for missionary work?
4. What has caused the great per capita decline of Christians in American cities over the past fifty years?
5. Why are potential pastors and missionaries reluctant to move to and serve in urban centers?

3

Principles of Urban Ministry, Part 1

Interpersonal Guidelines that Insure Success

On April 14, 1912, at 10:00 p.m., the Titanic crashed into an iceberg in the mid-Atlantic and four hours later sank. One woman in a lifeboat asked if she could go back to her room. She was given only three minutes to do so. She hurried down the corridors, already tilting dangerously, through the gambling room piled ankle-deep in money. In her room were her treasures waiting to be taken, but instead, she snatched up three oranges and hurried back to the boat. One hour before she would have naturally chosen diamonds over oranges, but in the face of death, what is of value is seen more clearly. Likewise, as we face death or perhaps after we experience a resurrected awareness of what is really important in life and ministry, we will see how important it is for our ministry to be rooted and filtered through a system of core values.

Values are often unwritten assumptions that guide our action. Values demonstrate our conviction and priorities and are confirmed by our actions, not just our words. Values are not a doctrinal statement but, rather, convictions that determine how our church operates. Values provide the foundation for formulating goals and setting the direction of the church's ministry. Core values are statements that affirm what is distinctive about a church.

In this chapter I would like to elaborate on three essential core values or principles of urban ministry that are foundational, insuring that we are following "Interpersonal Guidelines That Insure Success for the Kingdom of God."

PRINCIPLE ONE: URBAN MINISTRY MUST BE INCARNATIONAL

In John 20:21, at one of the resurrection appearances with the disciples, Jesus said "As the Father has sent Me, I also send you." There is much that can be said about how the Father sent Jesus and how we are to go in a similar manner. God sent our Lord to preach, to be persecuted, to suffer, to make known his will, and to offer salvation to mankind. But the divine plan of the incarnation also carries significant information as to the mode in which God sent his son to the earth.

In John 1:14 the gospel writer tells how Jesus' penetration into society serves as an example of true contextualization. He tells us, "And the Word became flesh, and dwelt among us." As Charles Lyons, Senior Pastor of Armitage Baptist Church in Chicago states it, "Jesus Christ moved into the neighborhood." He literally became one with the people; born as a Jewish child, having grown up in the Galilean town of Nazareth, raised "on the other side of the tracks" as it were, a town of poor reputation, indicated by Nathaniel's question to Philip: "Can any good thing come out of Nazareth?" (John 1:46).

It is astounding to think of the God of the universe invading earth and being incarnated as a helpless child, setting aside his divinity and becoming a baby. When he was hungry or when his diaper needed changing, his only recourse was to cry. He couldn't even swat mosquitoes from his body. He became a helpless infant, part of the Middle Eastern culture. As he grew, he had to develop as all other children. Luke tells us, "And Jesus kept increasing in wisdom and stature, and in favor with God and men" (Luke 2:52). He had to grow in wisdom because he emptied himself (Phil 2:6–7) of his knowledge of the Law and the Prophets. He had to learn as every other young Jewish boy. He had to grow in stature as his body grew physically, and he had to grow in favor with God and man. His growth "in favor with God" indicates a spiritual growth, not becoming sinless but seeking a deeper understanding, appreciation, and relationship with his Father. His growth "in favor with man" requires a social growth, which indicates that Jesus was well liked by those he knew. As a man he spoke the dialect of a Galilean, he ate the food that neighbors ate, he loved the customs that other Jewish men loved. He could have possessed another human body as demons do. He could have created a temporary body to indwell, a Christophany, as we see numerous times in the Old Testament. He didn't choose these methods but instead incarnated and became a real man, immersing himself into the culture of that day.

There was no aerial banner proclaiming God's plan of salvation. He didn't drop gospel tracts from the sky or blitz the world with Scripture portions. He studied the language, people, and culture for thirty years before he began his ministry. There were no shouts from heaven: "I love you!" There were no weekend evangelistic trips to the hood to share the gospel. Jesus did not commute from heaven. "The Word became flesh, and dwelt among us" (John 1:14). As Charles Lyons has said, "He came to the worst neighborhood in his universe, the neighborhood called Earth where his life would be taken." Jesus became part of this culture, and he came for the long haul, which lasted for thirty-three years until his death.

How should the example of Jesus and his incarnation impact our ministry? Jesus said, "As my Father hath sent me, even so send I you" (John 20:21 KJV). God expects us to incarnate, as it were, in our neighborhood of the city. Of course, we are not able to attain a literal incarnation, but we can, to the best of our ability, become part of the people we came to reach. That means several things:

First of all, that the missionary or pastor should move into the general area of the people he serves. In urban ministry we cannot commute.

For too long, men and women have lived in some comfortable neighborhood or suburb, commuting to the city or their target neighborhood for ministry. There may be some who make true salvation decisions as a result, but few of these converts will ever be discipled. Most will never attend a Bible-believing church and if they grow at all, it may take years before they get the very basics of how to be a follower of Jesus. Those that commute will not have a real sense of appreciation and understanding of the people they are serving, and they will not have the credibility they need to effectively reach and disciple them.

Second, to be incarnate means that we will become a part of the people, studying the culture and language of the inhabitants we are trying to reach. This culture may not only be different ethnically, but there is also the urban culture as well as social and economic elements that make each person unique. To truly understand the people one must rub shoulders day in and day out, to share in their culture, living where they live.

Third, being incarnate means that we will plant our roots and plan to stay for the long haul (more on longevity in the next chapter). By doing this we will develop love for the people, and the people will begin to love us as we grow "in favor" with the people we are serving.

PRINCIPLE TWO: URBAN MINISTRY MUST BE INTENTIONAL

Jesus did everything with intentionality. His days began early and ended late. Everything he said had a divine purpose, and everywhere he went fit into the divine plan. Jesus intentionally chose twelve disciples, as written in Luke 6:13, after a full night of prayer. It was not by chance that he spent so much of his short ministry discipling these twelve men so they could follow his example. Jesus intentionally chose to go to a forbidden city in a forbidden region to demonstrate that the new order would be to cross all ethnic boundaries to reach the world. He chose not to bypass Samaria but to go directly through that region to establish a cross-cultural ministry there. After leading the woman at the well to himself in Sychar, he spent several days (John 4:40) with his disciples in that Samaritan city instructing the new believers and leading more people to himself. It was not by chance that his last words on earth were the command for his followers to make disciples of all nations (Matt 28:19–20; Acts 1:8). It was not the luck of the draw that he died as prophesized, rose from the dead as predicted, ascended into heaven as planned, and that he will come back at the time appointed. Intentionality was the deliberate plan of everything Jesus did and is the approach of every effective ministry completed in his name. The key to intentional ministry is choosing the right things to be intentional about.

We must be intentional in our approach to Scriptures. We should teach all of God's Word as the literal, inspired rule of faith and practice. Without dutiful compliance to God's Word, ministry becomes aimless and may have no more eternal impact than a social club or benevolent charity.

In urban ministry we must be intentional as to our location. It would have been much easier for Armitage to purchase a building in the suburbs twenty-nine years ago instead of the building they bought in the heart of the inner city of Chicago. Real estate was cheaper, cost of living lower, the incomes of our parishioners would have been higher, and the social problems to deal with would have been less intense. Realtors brought appealing opportunities, but their conviction was to stay in the city facing the greatest need. To move to the suburbs meant that they would have had to abandon the people they were committed to reach.

We must be intentional about evangelism. A number of years ago I met with a major Christian relief agency and a number of inner city ministries. The agency wanted to pump a sizable amount of money into the city to augment their urban effort. For several hours each organization shared how they could use the money for their various ministries: food pantries, homeless shelters, job training programs, and so on. I asked the moderator where evangelism fit into these urban plans. The moderators quickly replied, "We assume evangelism is taking place." If I have learned anything from my twenty-nine years of ministry, it is that evangelism doesn't just happen. There must be a plan and relentless effort to make evangelism central to our ministries. The social tools listed above like food pantries, homeless shelters, and job training programs are important ministries but they must be tools or bridges to reach a higher purpose of introducing the patron to Jesus Christ who offers them eternal salvation.

There are millions of people in the city that need Christ. We have to intentionally train people and weave into our programs a methodology that fosters evangelism. One of the tools our church has adopted to encourage evangelism is our "Ten Most Wanted List." We have printed cards with ten numbered lines under the "Ten Most Wanted" heading. We encouraged our people to keep a list of those they most want to see come to Christ. We ask them to pray over each person on a regular basis and then ask God for an opportunity to share Christ with them. We also encourage our people to list results on the prayer/praise portion of the Welcome Card in our pew racks. This effort is promoted for five or six months allowing for occasional testimonies and the sharing of results. After a time, we end the program so the effort will not become too old and mundane. We use this tool every three or four years and have found that efforts like this have yielded great results with many people coming to a saving knowledge of Jesus Christ.

Intentionality is also necessary for discipleship. As I emphasized in the chapter I titled "The Mother of All Challenges," most churches across our nation are not doing a very good job in the area of discipleship because we intentionally run programs but do not offer biblical discipleship. This is indeed bizarre because discipleship is the commission of the church. No one will be discipled unless we intentionally disciple them. Just inviting them to church is not enough. You need a plan and you need to intentionally and persistently work the plan. In the city one of the most powerful and necessary ministries is one-on-one and small group discipleship. Because of the transient nature of the city, along with the wicked environment, we need to work with people with an in-depth intensity. Discipleship is the only truly effective method.

We must be intentional in church planting. We shouldn't leave all the urban church planting to mission agencies. There is a great need for vibrant churches in cities all around the world. In this country there is a great need because of the vacuum created by so many believers who fled from the cities to the suburbs in the '60s, '70s, and '80s. So far Armitage has planted three congregations and has goals of launching many more churches in the upcoming years. If we believe that the church is God's ordained institution for accomplishing his plan, we need to intentionally create and expand these initiatives in whatever way we can.

We must be intentional in training people for urban ministry. One of the great needs of urban ministry is for training centers where students can be trained on site. If you become a foreign missionary, you are trained in school and by the agency you serve under. Why is it that we think we can come to a large urban area that, in many respects, is a foreign mission field, without going through field training? In the city we work with multiple ethnic cultures and with unique pressures and problems. For years we have operated an internship program called our C.A.U.S.E. Program (Chicago Armitage Urban Study Experience). Through this program students can come for a three-month or a one-year internship. Our goal is to provide better understanding of urban ministry through a hands-on approach, improving the success rate of those entering an urban field. It takes intentionality to provide that kind of training.

We should intentionally provide a presence in the community. When Christ ministered on earth he didn't stay in the temple. His time was spent with the people. At the church where I pastor, we intentionally try to minister outside of the four walls of our building. For example:

1. We plan Prayer Walks in the summer during our Wednesday Prayer Meeting. We send our members out in groups of twos or threes to walk through the neighborhood and pray for whatever needs they see.

2. When someone is shot in our part of the city we organize a rally in cooperation with the police department. These rallies are held at the location where the crime was committed, giving us an opportunity to show our support for the police department and urge participation of the neighbors to divulge any information that might help the apprehension of the guilty parties. We have, at times, even provided a financial reward for anyone providing information leading to the apprehension and conviction of the guilty person. This effort shows the neighborhood that we are concerned about them. We are not a group of people cooped up in our building caring only about our own needs.

3. We have outdoor meetings several times each summer. One of the meetings held in front of the church is called our Parade of Miracles in which we feature the salvation stories of some of our members along with a contemporary worship service, conducted outside for our neighbors to observe. Another outside service we have conducted for years is our Back-to-School Rally where we send our kids back to school with a mission and with our prayers. At this rally we have many drawings in which we give back-to-school gifts, many of which are provided by area merchants. We also have a special outdoor baptismal service every August at a park pond called the Humboldt Park Lagoon located two miles south of our church. This service includes an outdoor praise service with baptismal candidates sharing their salvation testimonies for believers and non-believers to hear.

4. We minister in the neighborhood to children and single moms through our A.R.M.S. Ministry (Armitage Reaching Many Souls), which includes Bible studies for single women and children. A.R.M.S. also provides camp ministries for the kids and a transportation service to and from church.

5. Chicago Hope, our mercy ministry is held outside the church in a community center building providing a food pantry three times each week, an after-school program, an English as a Second Language class, job training, Children's Computer Camp, Health Fare, Thanksgiving and Christmas dinners, and a Thanksgiving basket and Christmas gift distribution for families in need.

Anything that is worth doing needs intentionality both in planning and in implementation.

PRINCIPLE THREE: URBAN MINISTRY MUST BE PERSONAL

Our society is becoming increasingly impersonal. More and more of the daily activities that used to involve contact with another human being are being automated. When we make a telephone call we often talk to a digitized voice mail. When we go to the gas station we pay at the pump. At many retail outlets we now go through the do-it-yourself checkout lane where we scan our items and don't even make contact with a cashier. Today the ATM has replaced the bank teller. Modern man, perhaps more now than at any time in history, has a need to be connected. What we all want is to be understood on a deep, fundamental level, and not only understood, but accepted.

Why do human beings have such an innate relational need and why is it so important to effective ministry?

First, our God is a personal God. God's character, unlike so many things in our world today, is personal. He remembers our history, he's aware of our flaws, he grieves over our sins, and yet he loves us with an eternal, unchanging, and unbounded love. There's nothing like it in the universe. His love for us is absolute, and his love for us is personal. Because God is personal, he relates to us in a personal way; not merely as a part of creation, not just as members of a group, but also as individuals. Psalm 139:1–12 demonstrates that God's knowledge of us is absolutely comprehensive, in every conceivable way. He always knows where we are and knows exactly what we're doing. There is literally nowhere that we can go, in heaven or on earth, where he will be unable to observe us. Moreover, he knows how we think. Of the Lord the psalmist writes, "you understand my thought from afar" and "Even before there is a word on my tongue, Behold, O Lord, You know it all." In other words, he knows what we're going to say before we say it.

One of the reasons he knows us so well is that he is the one who made us. Psalm 139:13–16 tells us that he's the one who knit us together in our mother's wombs. You can't get much more personal than that. In fact, it's not even accurate to say that God first came to know us at conception because he knew us before we were ever conceived. He knew us as his precious children even before the world came into existence. Even prayer is an act of communion with a personal God. If God is anything, he is personal.

Second, we were created as personal beings. We can live only in relationships. We need each other. A rather crude and cruel experiment was carried out by Emperor Frederick, who ruled the Roman Empire in the thirteenth century. He wanted to know what man's original language was: Hebrew, Greek, or Latin. He decided to isolate a few infants from the sound of the human voice. He reasoned that they would eventually speak the natural tongue of man. Wet nurses who were sworn to absolute silence were obtained, and though it was difficult for them, they abided by the rule. The infants never heard a word—not a sound from a human voice. Within several months they were all dead.[1]

Humankind needs personal interaction. We are created in God's image as personal beings with intellect, emotions, and will. As we read the account of man's creation, it is interesting to note that God put everything in the garden to make it a paradise—all types of fruit and vegetables, every kind of animal that God had instructed Adam to name. He lived in absolute bliss yet something was missing. Adam was created as a personal being. He needed another human being to whom to relate. In Genesis 2:18 we read that "the Lord God said, 'It is not good for the man to be alone; I will make him a helper suitable for him.'" But just having a helper was not good enough. God ordained marriage and made them one flesh. Then God told Adam and Eve to be fruitful and multiply and fill the earth, filling the earth with relational beings.

God not only ordained marriage but he also ordained the local church (Matt 16:18; Eph 1:22; 5:23) to accomplish his purpose in this age. God put relational beings in a secondary relationship structure. Then he told us to encourage each other, build each other up. He said when you have sinned to first confess it to God then go to the person you have offended and confess it to him. He wants us to seek reconciliation (Matt 5:24). You see God is all about relationships, and he made us personal beings and put us in a relational environment. We were created as personal beings.

Third, the personal approach is the most effective approach to ministry. We relate to each other in a personal way. If we are going to be effective as a church—if we are going to be effective in our ministry—our church and our ministry must be personal.

1. Beadle, *Mind*, 53.

Evangelism and discipleship are prime examples of the need for personal ministry. The most effective approach for evangelism is the personal approach. Witnessing with a form letter or gospel tract is not as effective as a personal, hand-signed letter. A personal letter is not as effective as talking to a person face-to-face. Does that mean we should not hand out tracts? Of course not. We do, however, need to make the tracts as personal as possible. We need to place our church name, address, and phone number on the back and give the tract with friendly words of introduction. Sharing your previously developed salvation testimony is also very effective because it is personal.

The world will not be won to Christ by a non-personal method like mass evangelism or through Internet web sites. We can use those methods but we need to focus our attention on the most effective method. The same is true of discipleship.

Jesus knew he had a short window of opportunity. As it turned out, he only had three-and-a-half years to revolutionize the world, providing redemption for all mankind. He didn't use modern technology. What did Jesus do? He poured his life into twelve men whom he discipled. They were not of the elite of their day, most of them had no money; many of the disciples were uneducated, and some had major character flaws. He chose them not based on their money or talent but based on what they could become. And we are to follow his example by teaching the same message and using the same methodology.

Fourth, the personal approach is the basis for personal ministry. How do you reach people of other cultures and background? How do you reach a drug addict or alcoholic? How do you reach your world's worst enemy? You do it by a personal demonstration of love. Demonstrating love is the key to personal ministry. When people know we love them, their lives are touched. Love is the universal language. It spans race and language. It is the primary tool the Holy Spirit uses to reach and change people.

In urban ministry we must never emphasize the impersonal but the personal approach to ministry. Small group Bible studies held in homes are an important way to have a personal ministry in the lives of your people, and it is especially important as a church grows in numbers. Also, every pastor and urban minister should put a lifelong emphasis on one-on-one ministry to a few individuals at a time. This personal ministry will have a lifelong impact on its recipients. (There is more on the biblical approach to love in the chapter "Reaching the Disenfranchised, Part 2" under the section titled "Develop a Personal Ministry"). Please read on for other principles of urban ministry in the next chapter.

REVIEW QUESTIONS

1. How should Jesus' example of incarnation influence our philosophy of urban ministry?
2. What are three ways we can make our ministries incarnational?
3. List seven things the author states we need to do in order to be intentional.
4. Especially since we live in a technological culture, why is it strategic that the focus of our ministry be personal?
5. Why is the personal approach the most effective approach to ministry?

4

Principles of Urban Ministry, Part 2

Guidelines that Insure Credibility

There is a tale told of that great English actor Macready. An eminent preacher once said to him: "I wish you would explain to me something." "Well, what is it? I don't know that I can explain anything to a preacher," replied Macready. The preacher asked, "What is the reason for the difference between you and me? You are appearing before crowds night after night with fiction, and the crowds come wherever you go. I am preaching the essential and unchangeable truth, and I am not getting any crowd at all." Macready's answer was this: "This is quite simple. I can tell you the difference between us. I present my fiction as though it were truth; you present your truth as though it were fiction."[1]

What a scathing indictment of many believers. Credibility is absolutely necessary if we will ever have an impact on those we want to reach. In a world with so many religious frauds we must make sure that we as individuals, and our ministries, display absolute integrity in our lives and all of our dealings. In this chapter I would like to talk about four additional principles of urban ministry that relate to our credibility.

PRINCIPLE FOUR: URBAN MINISTRY MUST BE CROSS-CULTURAL

You have heard it said that the Sunday morning service is the most segregated hour in America. We will never have credibility until the church treats all men with love and respect. God loves diversity as demonstrated in his creation. We see it in the thousands of different types of flowers, shrubs, and trees. We see it in the variety of animal life such as fish, birds,

1. Morgan, *Preaching*, 36.

reptiles, and so on. Every human is a unique creation, different in appearance, personality, and life experience. We also see God's love for variety in the number of ethnic groups, each one different in appearance and culture. God loves every people, tribe, and nation, and this great diversity has been his design from the beginning: creating mankind in his image.

In the book of Jonah we see God's love for nationalities other than his chosen people. In this account, which Jesus attests to as historical (Matt 12:40–41), God demonstrates his grace) the gospel of forgiveness through repentance) to one of the greatest group of enemies of his people. God sent Jonah as a missionary to one of the most ruthless people in the known world, the Assyrians living in Nineveh, one of the largest cities in that country located in modern day Iraq. Jonah hated the Assyrians and wanted no part in their reconciliation with God. Reluctantly, he preached the gospel to them resulting in full repentance. Why did the outcome of revival seem to vanish without a historical trace? Perhaps it was because there had been no discipleship. If the people had been taught about God and had grown spiritually, there would have been no need for God's judgment on Nineveh in 612 B.C. Nevertheless, God demonstrated his love and concern for the greatest enemies of his people, a group who had a reputation for mercilessly persecuting their Jewish captives.

Jesus told his disciples, "But you will receive power when the Holy Spirit has come upon you; and you shall be My witnesses both in Jerusalem, and in all Judea and Samaria, and even to the remotest part of the earth" (Acts 1:8). The Great Commission included going to the people groups (the Samaritans) you don't feel comfortable with, as well as to every part of the earth. In Matthew 28:19, Jesus told his disciples to make disciples of all nations. The Greek word for nations is *ethnos* and denotes a race or tribe, specifically a foreign (non-Jewish) one. This is where we get the word ethnicity. Jesus was not telling us to go to every nation or country. He was saying we were to disciple every people group. God's plan is for his people to go beyond their own kind to people of other cultures.

As previously noted, Jesus himself went to people of a different culture in John 4. Jesus only had three years to establish his massive movement, and he spent two days of it with the hated Samaritans in the city of Sychar (John 4:39–41). Because the people of Samaria were half Jewish and half Assyrian, no good Jew would have anything to do with them. They wouldn't ever pass through their towns. Our Savior, though he was Jewish, purposely went through Samaria (John 4:4) to bring good news to people of a mixed ethnic birth. John 4:40 tells us that Jesus stayed there for two additional days and led many others to himself and instructed the new believers.

Later, after the church began, Philip, one of the original deacons, went to Samaria and led many to Christ (Acts 8:4–13). When the apostles heard about the new believers in Samaria, they sent Peter and John who laid hands on them and the Samaritans received the Holy Spirit—kind of a Samaritan Pentecost. Following Jesus' admonition in Acts 1:8, Peter and John went to many Samaritan villages and preached the gospel. This entire story illustrates God's compassion for reaching men and women from other cultures.

In the midst of the Samaritan revival, an angel of the Lord told Phillip to go to the desert road that leads to Gaza (Acts 8:25–40). On this road he saw an Ethiopian eunuch who was on his chariot heading home. The Ethiopian was undoubtedly a black man who came almost two thousand miles from home to Israel. Philip shared the gospel with him; he believed and was baptized. According to tradition, the Ethiopian went back, taking the gospel to his homeland and becoming the "'father' of the church in Ethiopia. Tradition tells us that he fathered the Coptic Church, which is the oldest expression of Christianity that survives to this day, and traces its roots directly back to the first century and this eunuch."[2] His conversion illustrates that Christ's love for the lost transcends national boundaries and, in this case, embraces one whose physical mutilation would have excluded him from full participation in Judaism (Lev 21:20; Deut. 23:1).

God's plans for our future will be cross-cultural. Revelation 7:9–10 proclaims, "After these things I looked, and behold, a great multitude which no one could count, from every nation [the word nation is the Greek word *ethnos*, as we discussed earlier as in Matt 28:19] and all tribes and peoples and tongues, standing before the throne and before the Lamb, clothed in white robes, and palm branches were in their hands; and they cry out with a loud voice, saying, 'Salvation to our God who sits on the throne, and to the Lamb.'" Our eternity will be cross-cultural because our Savior called them, died for them, and used one of his servants to lead them to himself.

2. Gage, *Ethiopian*.

The first example of a multicultural church was at Antioch where Barnabas built a multicultural pastoral team that, according to Ray Bakke, was the "first large city-center church we know anything about [that] had a five person pastoral team from three continents. Antioch was the third largest city in the empire, after Rome and Alexandria, with between 500,000 and 800,000 residents."[3]

The city is a foreign mission field with every ethnic group residing in mass numbers. As Ray Bakke stated, "Missions is no longer about crossing the oceans, jungles, and deserts, but about crossing the streets of the world's cities."[4] If we reach our cities with all their ethnic diversity, people will return to their country and impact will be seen through the world.

Cross-cultural means more than ethnic. It includes people with different economic levels, different sexual orientation, and people speaking different languages. On Sunday morning at Armitage Baptist Church it is common to see a Puerto Rican CEO sitting right next to a Puerto Rican gangbanger. They are from the same ethnic background but are from very different cultures. We have over forty-three different ethnic groups attending our services. If you add the other cultures represented by the homeless, homosexuals, and gang members, to name a few, you have an enormous diversity.

How do we reach people of different cultures? First, I think the key is to implement each of this chapter's core values or principles of urban ministry into your ministry. Second, we need to minister in love. It is love that motivates cross-cultural ministry. Genuine, demonstrated love will win acceptance and love from people of any culture. Third, it is important that we are culturally sensitive but not culturally driven. In other words, we need to be ourselves. We should not try to act like an African American or Hispanic, for example (assuming we are not from that ethnic group). If we are genuine and demonstrate love, they will accept us. Fourth, we should avoid thinking in terms of stereotypes because a stereotype does not give a true representation of the people of any ethnic group. Also, stereotypes are often demeaning. Fifth, we need to be intentional in affirming the culture of the people we are trying to reach. We affirm them by incorporating their cultural Christian music into our service. We also affirm their culture by involving them in our

3. Bakke, *Theology*, 146.

4. Ibid., 13.

ministry. When possible, they should be recruited to the Deacon Board, as well as full-time positions. They should serve as teachers, ushers, and greeters. We should recruit them to serve on our worship team, have them give announcements, and publicly read Scriptures. We should invite guest speakers who represent their culture, and make positive reference to elements of their culture in sermons. Sixth, if the people from the ethnic group you are trying to reach prefer another language, it is important to recruit people who speak their language. Our attitude will be demonstrated by our actions. There should never be a trace of prejudice. If there is, it will destroy your ministry.

Cross-cultural ministry is not a choice, it is a biblical mandate. Wherever we serve, we should be seeking how to reach our Samaria for God. God is bringing the world to our doorstep. Let's win them while there is time.

PRINCIPLE FIVE: URBAN MINISTRY MUST BE CHARACTERIZED BY CREDIBILITY AND INTEGRITY

In 2 Corinthians 2:17—3:2, the Apostle Paul tells us that our character should be demonstrated by our actions. If I have no credibility or integrity no one will listen to my message.

As a church, Armitage has always looked for ways to be responsive to community needs. A number of years ago, in the city of Chicago, there was a Public School teachers' strike that lasted several months. In our church building we organized an alternative school inviting students from the community to continue their education at our church, free of charge, during the strike. The effort was well received and very successful.

Not long after the school strike, a coalition of radical groups decided to hold demonstrations in commemoration of the one-year anniversary of the death of David Gunn, an abortion doctor in Pensacola, Florida. These demonstrations were to be held at a number of sites in several states. Armitage had developed a reputation as a leading church in Chicago in the pro-life movement, so our church was chosen as the Chicago location for the demonstration. The demonstration was set for a Wednesday evening, so our leadership decided to turn our mid-week service into a concert of prayer. A large African American church from the south side of Chicago bussed people to our church to join the prayer meeting. They brought a large youth choir that was stationed on our front steps to drown out the protesters. It wasn't long before the demonstrators slipped away, defeated and dejected. God gave us the victory.

Hundreds of leaflets had been passed out asking people to demonstrate against Armitage. We found out that representatives of the demonstrating groups had gone door-to-door asking neighborhood residents for help. Though few neighbors were in agreement with our Christian message, not one participated with the demonstrating groups. Repeatedly, our neighbors told the demonstrators that the people at Armitage were good people, that we were good for the community; we had credibility.

What destroys credibility and integrity? Some churches destroy their credibility and integrity by simply being inconsiderate neighbors. At Armitage, we work hard at preserving our reputation. As bad as we need parking during Sunday services, we do not let our people park in residential parking. We even shuttle people in vans to avoid taking residential parking from our neighbors. As a positive effort to maintain credibility, we often have visiting groups pick up litter over the entire block. We make every effort to be responsive to community needs, using our building as an election polling place and opening our doors, free of charge, for community meetings. We also provide a food pantry for people in need, as well as many other services.

To maintain credibility and integrity with the people we are serving, we always keep our word. When we schedule a meeting or program, we never cancel. We want a reputation that people can count on, knowing our programs will be held at the promised times and dates. When we recruit adults who work with children, we run background checks so that parents can be assured that no sexual offenders will find their way into our lay or professional staff.

Unlike most churches in this modern society, we practice church discipline and have seen it as a wonderful tool, restoring the prodigal back to Christ and at the same time helping to preserve the testimony of our church and the testimony of Christ. We seek to be honest in our dealings, including promotion—never embellishing stories with the media. Our reputation is important to us so we strive to maintain credibility and integrity with the world as well as the people we serve.

If you don't have credibility and integrity as a minister and as a church, you have no ministry. You won't be trusted, and the cause of Christ will suffer.

PRINCIPLE SIX: URBAN MINISTRY MUST BE CHARACTERIZED BY LONGEVITY

According to The Barna Group, the average pastor only stays five years in a church, even though the greatest ministry impact in a pastorate is in years five through fourteen.[5] I believe this short period of time is one of the reasons for little growth in evangelical churches. In urban ministry, longevity is even more critical. Many city dwellers have experienced an unstable life. Many may not know their father, their mother may have a temporary boyfriend, and for numerous reasons they may move from one apartment to the next. Their entire experience is unstable; therefore, they desperately need consistency and stability. The church needs to be a picture of stability, and the pastor and other church staff need to be a part of this stable picture.

Many who God has touched are non-believers or may have received Christ but, because of Satan's influence, have drifted away. As God continues to draw them to salvation, or as believers under God's corrective and chastening hand, they may eventually come back looking for the person who God used to impact their life. What if the person who has ministered to them completes his brief stint and moves on? Who will continue the process? The lack of longevity is an element of credibility in the eyes of those we are seeking to reach. People in ministry need to weather the storms, persevering in the same location. If we serve for an extended period of time in the same ministry, the blessings and the fruit that come from service will be far greater than for the worker or pastor who has many short-term ministries. It takes time to reach people and even longer to disciple them. You will begin to see fruit only after an extended period, usually years.

Most pastors never have the joy of seeing the children who are saved under their ministry grow up and become missionaries or serve as leaders in the church. What a joy to stay and see the fruit of your labors. No wonder church staff members are looked on as outsiders. They leave just as they are beginning to become known and accepted. How can a pastor truly become "incarnational" with such a short tenure? When the church members have seen pastors come and go, no wonder they often don't support the changes and programs "the new guy" brings in. We need to learn how to weather the storm, work through issues, dig in, and stay.

5. Barna, *Pastors*, 2001.

At the end of his life Paul said, "I have fought the good fight, I have finished the course, I have kept the faith" (2 Tim 4:7). Reaching people in the city requires a fight on our part. It requires determination to finish what we started, and it requires consistent labor through the power of the Holy Spirit if we are to see significant results.

What would have happened if Charles Lyons, instead of staying for thirty-six years, had left Armitage after five years? Having come to Armitage with only twenty-five people, how many would we have ended up with after five years? Seventy-five? One hundred? Is that why the average American church in 2000 had an average of ninety adults in Sunday morning attendance?[6] We must plan in terms of the long haul; we must fight the good fight of faith.

PRINCIPLE SEVEN: URBAN MINISTRY MUST BE SUPERNATURAL

Herbert Jackson told a class of students how, as a missionary, he was assigned a car that would not start without a push. After pondering his problem, he devised a plan. He went to the school near his home, got permission to take some children out of class, and had them push his car, so with the key on he could pop the clutch, and it would start. As he made his rounds, he would either park on a hill or leave the engine running.

Ill health forced the Jackson family to leave, and a new missionary came to that station. When Jackson proudly began to explain his arrangement for getting the car started, the new man began looking under the hood. Before the explanation was complete, the new missionary interrupted, "Why, Dr. Jackson, I believe the only trouble is this loose cable." He tightened the nut on the cable, stepped into the car, turned the key, and to Jackson's astonishment, the engine roared to life. For two years needless trouble could have been avoided. All he needed was consistent power. That's what we need isn't it? Consistent power. We tell the world, and rightly so, that we have a supernatural, all-powerful God. As such, we must remember this important truth: Even when our ministries seem to be dead and powerless, thereby losing our credibility in the eyes of those to whom we strive to minister, we still have the same Holy Spirit living in us. All we need to do is tap into his power.

6. Barna, *Attendance*, 3.

The best evidence is God's magnificent creation. Whether we study the planets and galaxies above or the plant or the animal world around us, God's creation is astonishing. Of course, the capstone of all of God's creation was the creation of man.

What keeps it together and running perpetually? In Acts 17:28 (KJV) the Bible says: "For in him we live and move and have our being." God is so great that we don't have the intellect to understand him or the vocabulary to explain him. And throughout the Old Testament this same God revealed himself in extraordinary and supernatural ways.

God also revealed himself to be supernatural in the New Testament period, after the Church was first organized, in the early stages of the Church Age. One of these remarkable stories is found in Acts 3 when Peter and John came upon a crippled man sitting by the temple gate. He had been crippled from his birth, was over forty years old (Acts 4:22), and had never walked.

This story of how this man was healed intrigued me so I did a little research, interviewing two physical therapists, one who was the head of the physical therapy department in a large Chicago hospital. I was interested in what would be involved in a healing of this nature. I explained my project and then asked if doctors had the ability to correct the physical or neurological cause, and what would be involved in the therapy necessary to bring the person to a normal recovery.

First, the therapist explained, it is probable that a person born as a paraplegic and growing to adulthood in that state would have undeveloped legs. To grow normally, our limbs have to be used. Therefore, his legs were probably very short and undeveloped. Not only would they be short, but the bones would be very weak and unable to support the weight of a forty-year-old man.

Second, his legs may also have been bent or twisted, especially if he sat on them for forty years. If he were to walk normally, the bones would probably have to be straightened.

Third, once the legs were in working order, it would be necessary for the man to go through painful, long-term, extensive therapy and exercise. The bones and muscles would have to be built up. The muscles in his legs would be small to non-existent. Like his bones, the muscles would be weak and would never hold his weight. Assuming the legs were normal in length and not twisted, it would take several years of hard work to build up strength and stamina, and even with all of the exercise and therapy, he most likely would not be perfectly normal.

Fourth, the man would have to learn to walk just like a one-year-old baby. He would have to develop the skill necessary to walk and leap.

Friends and family members would carry the cripple each day to this site where he sat to beg for money so that he could survive. Peter and John walked by and saw the crippled beggar sitting there with his undeveloped, shriveled legs. Peter stopped and focused on this needy man and said,

> 'I do not possess silver and gold, but what I do have I give to you: In the name of Jesus Christ the Nazarene—walk!' And seizing him by the right hand, he raised him up; and immediately his feet and his ankles were strengthened. With a leap he stood upright and began to walk; and he entered the temple with them, walking and leaping and praising God. And all the people saw him walking and praising God; and they were taking note of him as being the one who used to sit at the Beautiful Gate of the temple to beg alms, and they were filled with wonder and amazement at what had happened to him (Acts 3:6–10).

You see, when Peter told the man to walk in the name of Jesus, the man not only gained the healing he needed but he instantly had the strength of a normal man. His bones apparently were lengthened, thickened, strengthened, and straightened, and he automatically had the skill to walk and to leap. That is indeed supernatural!

The same God who created the universe and the same God who did his marvelous miracles for the children of Israel is the same God who supernaturally healed the crippled man. Who did he use to do this miraculous healing? He did it through Peter, a crude, impulsive, and uneducated man who just a few years before had made a living as a poor fisherman. An important observation is that this is not a story from the Old Testament period, it happened after the early church was organized, as recorded in the book of Acts.

Do we have the same God today who Peter had? Is he willing to demonstrate his supernatural power through us today? Does he want to? The answer to all of these questions is a resounding *yes*! He has the power, and he wants to demonstrate it today! I am not implying that God will use us to raise the dead or heal the crippled. What I am saying is that he wants to use us to have extraordinary impact in peoples' lives.

All churches must depend on God's supernatural power if the people are going to win and disciple the world for Jesus Christ, but the need is especially necessary in the urban church. In the cities the problems are more concentrated, the cost of living is higher, the average income is lower, and most urban churches have less staff than the average church of the same size in the suburbs.

If half of the people are in the cities, where will the missionaries and pastors come from if they don't come from the cities? *God, we need your help. We can't do this unless you show yourself to be supernatural.*

God has continually worked supernaturally through the church where I serve. At Armitage, I see the Holy Spirit working through our church and people in great and amazing ways. A couple of years ago we bought a piece of property near the church to use for parking. The owner wanted over $1,000,000 for the property. After Pastor Lyons talked to the owner, he decided to sell the property to Armitage for $900,000 and to also give Armitage a $300,000 gift. During the two years we owned the property, we rented the space out which covered almost all we needed for the payment.

The city of Chicago contacted us to let us know that they were going to buy the property from us so they could build a public library on the site. After negotiations, we sold the property for $950,000. That means with the $300,000 gift and the profit on the sale, God blessed us with $350,000 profit on a piece of property we purchased for $100,000 less than the asking price.

But that's not the end of the story. The city of Chicago agreed to pay the expenses of bringing the property up to code, resurfacing it. They added to the contract that we have exclusive rights to use the parking lot free of charge during closed hours as long as the church exists. The city would maintain the lot which included all snow plowing.

The reason we bought the lot in the first place was for parking. God gave us parking with no maintenance and a $350,000 gift besides. We have a great and awesome God! He is supernatural!

In Ephesians 3:20–21 the Apostle Paul said, "Now to him who is able to do far more abundantly beyond all that we ask or think, according to the power that works within us."

The word *think* includes our imagination. This means that God is able to do super-abundantly more than you can think or even imagine because it is according to the power (in proportion to the power) who works in us. Of course, that is the infinite power of the Holy Spirit. It was the same power who created the universe, the same power who did the magnificent wonders for Israel, and it was the same power who raised the crippled man, through Peter.

Some may think that God is able but he won't do it! That was then and this is now! God is not playing with us. He is able and willing; in fact, he desires to do great things through each of us.

I think the average believer rarely sees the supernatural working of God through their life. Why is this? Perhaps the reason is found in the illustration I shared earlier about Herbert Jackson's car. This car had all the ability to function the way the manufacturer made it to function. The power was there all the time. Only a loose connection kept Jackson from putting that power to work.

I would like to "look under the hood" and see if the average Christian life has a loose connection. The Christian life is supposed to work to produce Spirit-energized saints. However, there are four potential weaknesses in your Christian life where God's power will be interrupted.

First, power interruption occurs when we do not take advantage of God's revelation as found in his Word. It's sad when you realize that most Christians don't read God's Word.

In one of his research surveys George Barna asked adult, "born-again" Christians what would make them spiritually successful. Only seven percent said that reading the Bible, and doing what the Bible says, is necessary for being spiritually successful.[7]

Did you know there are thousands of promises in the Bible? Herbert Lockyer listed eight thousand in his book, *All the Promises of the Bible*.[8] A great number of the promises are conditional. That means we have to meet the condition if we expect God to bless us with the promise. Most believers don't know what those promises and conditions are. No wonder God is not blessing and answering our prayers. No wonder we are living defeated lives. Nevertheless, the Bible is packed full of principles telling us how to live the Christian life.

Most believers are in dire financial straits because they haven't studied and put into practice God's principles of finance. Many Christian marriages are in trouble because they haven't studied and practiced principles that God laid out on how to be a Christian husband or wife.

If you are not studying God's Word on a regular and consistent basis, and obeying its principles and precepts, you will not have a successful

7. Barna, *Disciples*, 41.

8. Lockyer, *Promises,* front cover.

Christian life. If you spend as little time with your earthly fiancé or wife as you spend with your heavenly fiancé, your earthy marriage will never make it. In 2 Timothy 2:15, Paul urged Timothy, a young pastor to "[b]e diligent to present yourself approved to God as a workman who does not need to be ashamed, accurately handling the word of truth." Obedience to God's word is necessary if we desire to experience his blessings on our lives (Joshua 1:8).

Second, power interruption occurs when we do not respond to God's Word by faith. Faith is not a feeling. It's not something you get psyched up for. A feeling may be a by-product, but the feeling is not the faith. Faith is a decision to take God at his word and to act upon it. We are not talking about a gift of faith. We are talking about the way God requires that we respond to him. You make a decision to believe what God says and to take the necessary action to put it into practice. A simple study of Hebrews 11 will indicate that each one of the men and women listed in this great Hall of Faith made a decision to act. Faith is always demonstrated by action. If it is not practiced, it is not real faith. Hebrews 11:6 says, "nd without faith it is impossible to please Him." We will never experience God's power in our life if we don't begin practicing a faith life.

God wants to show himself to be great and powerful through you. He wants to make each of us men and women of faith. That's why he said in Matthew 17:20 that "[i]f you have faith the size of a mustard seed, you will say to this mountain, 'Move from here to there,' and it will move; and nothing will be impossible to you." He's not telling us we can rearrange the landscape. But he is telling us that God will respond to your faith in a supernatural way and you will experience his power working through you.

Third, power interruption occurs when we do not respond to people with love as commanded in God's Word. The Greek word here for love is *agapao*. We usually call it *agape* love. In Matthew 22:37–40 Jesus quoted Deuteronomy 6:5 and used the word *agapao* when he said, "'You shall love the Lord your God with all your heart, and with all your soul, and with all your mind.' This is the great and foremost commandment. The second is like it, 'You shall love your neighbor as yourself.' On these two commandments depend the whole Law and the Prophets."

What is *agape* love? Just as faith is not a feeling, *agape* love is not a feeling either. To love God with *agape* love is to treat God as your sovereign Lord and make decisions to do the right thing toward him. The right thing I must do toward God is to obey him. He says on these two commands hang all the law and the prophets. In other words, if I love God with all my heart, soul, and mind I won't need the law and the prophets. I will make decisions to obey God throughout the day. I will hate sin because my sin offends the God I love.

Fourth, the last power interruption, is depending on self and not on God. One of the sins that grieves God most is when his servants become arrogant and self-sufficient. When we serve him with that "I can do it" attitude, we leave little room for God's power. I can preach a sermon or teach a lesson but if God is not speaking through me, the time is wasted. No one will be changed and life will not be impacted for eternity. It is when I empty myself of this attitude and declare my total dependence on God and yield to the Spirit's control, that he shows up and demonstrates his power. If anything lasting results from our ministry, it will be because of him, not us. The longer I am in the ministry, the more I realize the importance of being totally dependent on him. That means I need to bathe what I do in prayer so God can work through me. And that is why we are here in the first place. I long for God to use me. I want him to do the supernatural through my life and ministry. As we obey and serve our great God, may we follow the admonition of the extraordinary missionary William Carey who said, "Expect great things from God; attempt great things for God."

REVIEW QUESTIONS

1. What New Testament passages indicate God's directive in reaching people from other cultures?
2. What are the six important suggestions for reaching people of different cultures?
3. What are important ingredients in maintaining and developing our credibility and integrity?
4. What are the benefits of staying in a ministry for the long haul?
5. What are the four weaknesses the author calls "power interruptions" that block God's supernatural power in our ministry?

5

Calibrating Our Compass

The Great Omission of the Great Commission

Life without purpose is barren indeed
There can't be a harvest unless you plant seed
There can't be attainment unless there's a goal
And man's but a robot unless there's a soul.
If we send no ships out, no ships will come in,
And unless there's a contest, nobody can win.
For games can't be won unless they are played,
And prayers can't be answered unless they are prayed.

—Author unknown

In Lewis Carroll's classic novel, *Alice's Adventures in Wonderland,* Alice seeks directions from the "Cheshire-Puss":

"Would you tell me, please, which way I ought to go from here?"

"That depends a good deal on where you want to get to," said the cat.

"I don't much care where—" said Alice.

"Then it doesn't matter which way you go," said the cat.

"—so long as I get *somewhere,*" Alice added as an explanation.

"Oh, you're sure to do that," said the cat, "if you only walk long enough."[1]

Just going somewhere might have been good enough for Alice, but it's not enough for us, especially concerning our ministry. Doing good and even accomplishing what may seem to be noble and right is not nec-

1. Carroll, *Wonderland*, 49.

essarily God's direction. As we look at the history of the church, one may ask where the church has been trying to go for the last sixteen hundred or so years. It is sure we have gone *somewhere*; but where does God expect us to go? What is the target we are aiming for? Could we be shooting at the wrong target? If we eventually get there, how much longer will it take us? I believe a close examination of God's directive will show that we have either misunderstood or misapplied God's greatest command to the church—the "great omission" of the Great Commission.

First of all, it is necessary to determine God's *purpose* for this age. This is the general aim God wants us to achieve. Second, what is God's *plan* or focused objective to insure that the church can accomplish this purpose? Finally, once we agree on a plan, we can come to the biblical *procedure* for accomplishing his plan discussed in the next chapter. Once we "calibrate our compass," we can expect God to do amazing things through a committed and prayerful church.

GOD'S PURPOSE FOR THIS AGE

What is God's *purpose* for this age? There are some who have quickly responded that it is God's purpose to Christianize the world. Proponents of this view may cite 2 Peter 3:9, where it says: "The Lord . . . is not wishing for any to perish but for all to come to repentance." Winning people to Christ is, of course, God's desire, but is it his purpose? Assuming we agree that God is sovereign and that he has never failed and will never fail in accomplishing his will, we can look at world statistics to see if God has, in fact, accomplished this purpose.

The history of the church is full of religion, but the number of true believers in Jesus Christ is far below the total number of people classified as Christians. In 1990 thirty percent of the world was classified as Christian. Out of that total 960 million were Roman Catholic and nearly 550 million were protestant. Of the protestant numbers there were 150 million classified as evangelical Christians. This means that the evangelical Christians composed of ten percent of the total population. All of these figures are considered conservative estimates.[2] Only God knows how many true believers are in the world today, but after giving his life to the study of Church history, the famous Kenneth Scott Latourette concluded that, "the course of Christianity on the planet has only recently begun is evident."[3]

2. Cairns, *Through the Centuries*, 505.
3. Latourette, *A History of Christianity*, 1476.

Is God a failure? If God's purpose were to save the world, we would have to conclude that he has been a miserable failure because the vast majority of people in every generation have not become believers. In fact, millions in every age have never seen a Bible and have never heard the plan of salvation. Proverbs 19:21 says, "[m]any are the plans in the mind of a man, but it is the purpose of the LORD that will stand" (ESV). It is certain that God will never fail at what he has chosen to accomplish.

What is God's purpose for this age? There are others who have responded that God's purpose is to evangelize the world, giving everyone in the world the gospel so that they have a choice to believe. Proponents of this view could cite Mark 16:15, which says: "And he said to them, 'Go into all the world and preach the gospel to all creation.'"

It is true that God has told us to preach the gospel. If we don't exercise our spiritual muscle, we will get flabby, and we have a lot of spiritually flabby Christians; but is it God's purpose in this age for the church to evangelize the world? God always accomplishes his purpose, but simple research into history will indicate whether or not world evangelization has ever taken place.

Christianity had a great beginning led by the apostles and their followers around AD 32 and ending AD 70. The ending of this period was marked by the destruction of Jerusalem led by Titus, the Roman General. During this time there was a great expansion of Christianity.

From AD 70 to AD 313 there continued to be good progress. At the time of the alleged conversion of Constantine, at the beginning of the fourth century, the number of Christians may have reached ten or twelve million. This estimate of believers was about one-tenth of the total population of the Roman Empire, with some estimates being higher.4 After AD 313, when Constantine signed the Edict of Milan, Christianity became legal. Nevertheless, the church accomplished very little after this period to achieve world evangelization.

From AD 476 to AD 1517, there were 1,041 very dark years of church history. AD 476 marks the fall of the Roman Empire and AD 1517 was the year Martin Luther tacked the Ninety-five Theses on the Castle Church door in Wittenberg. This period was marked with detestable acts endorsed and perpetuated by the Roman Catholic Church. This period includes the Spanish Inquisition with its many martyrs. It was the period in which the Catholic Church sold indulgences (or the

4. Schaff, *History*, 198.

selling of grace) so people could insure less time in purgatory. Many were saved, but this period could not be called a period of widespread evangelization.

AD 1700 marked the beginning of the great missions movement when Christianity really began taking hold. In fact, it wasn't until the nineteenth century when the protestant movement really structured themselves for mission expansion. "The Roman Catholic Church, between 1500 and 1700, won more converts in the pagan world than it lost to Protestants in Europe."[5] As you can conclude, there has never been a period when world evangelization has taken place or a time when evangelism even came close to being worldwide.

Evangelization of the World

AD 32 – AD 70 – a great beginning
AD 70 – AD 313 – continued progress
AD 476 – AD 1517 – weak evangelization
AD 1700 – Christianity began taking hold

Because of the millions of people in every age who never heard the gospel, evangelization, though a necessary part of the process, cannot be God's purpose. His purpose for this age is declared in Matthew 16:18 where Jesus said: "I will build My church; and the gates of Hades will not overpower it." There are five observations we can make as we analyze this statement. First of all, Christ is doing the building; Jesus says he will build his church. I am not building the church; I am simply a conduit or channel. Jesus is the builder. Second, the building was yet in the future from the moment he made the statement. He, of course, began building his church fifty days after his resurrection on the Day of Pentecost. Third, he is building his church. It is not my church; it is his church. Fourth, Hades itself (meaning death, perhaps even his death) will not stop the process. Fifth, God's plan, though not begun at the time Jesus spoke the words recorded in Matthew 16:18, is destined to succeed. God will never fail at what he determines to do. God's purpose will be achieved.

5. Kane, *Missions*, 259.

GOD'S PLAN FOR THE CHURCH

Since we have concluded that it is God's purpose to build his church, let us narrow the focus. What is God's plan to accomplish his purpose?

The disciples gathered on the Mount of Olives and after seeing the resurrected Lord they fell down on their faces and worshipped him. After a few moments of worship, Jesus gave his final instructions. These were the marching orders for the church. These parting words form directives from Jesus known as the Great Commission.

In Matthew 28:19–20, Jesus said, "Go therefore and make disciples of all the nations, baptizing them in the name of the Father and the Son and the Holy Spirit, teaching them to observe all that I commanded you; and lo, I am with you always, even to the end of the age."

Often missionary speakers preach from this passage telling us that God's command for us is to go. As we look at this passage more closely, we will discover that the command is not to "go" or to "baptize" or even to "teach." The *Greek* grammar indicates that the imperative is to "make disciples." The words "go," "baptizing," and "teaching" are adverbial participles, which modify the command "make disciples." An adverbial participle is a word that looks like a verb, but acts like an adverb. Therefore, the words "go," "baptize," and "teach" are words that tell us how we are to follow the imperative to "make disciples." It would be correct to translate this command as "going" or "in your going," "make disciples."

The disciples had just fallen on their faces in worship. The natural and only correct response of true heartfelt worship is service. Telling the disciples to "go" was unnecessary; they just finished worshipping the resurrected Lord. Jesus knew they were going to go, all the disciples needed was direction. Therefore, he gave the Great Commission to "make disciples."

Notice the command is not to merely make converts. I like the way Christopher Adsit put it when he said, "In a spiritual sense, we have a tendency to think that the greatest thing we Christians can do is beget babies. Consequently, what we have here in America today is the largest spiritual nursery in history."[6] It's important to note, however, that discipleship in no way devalues the importance of evangelism. On the contrary, the command includes evangelism. You cannot make a disciple of Christ unless he has been won to Christ, but you can lead many

6. Adsit, *Disciplemaking*, 72.

people to Christ without ever making a disciple. The problem has to do with our purpose. As I quoted earlier from the novel *Alice's Adventure in Wonderland*, it seems that many only try to "get *somewhere*." In following God's command, "somewhere" is not good enough. It is God's plan for the church to make mature disciples as spelled out in the verses above.

Because obedience to the Commission is so important, we need to reflect on how the church is doing in obeying the most important command ever uttered. Studies demonstrate that few churches are doing effective discipleship. Christian Researcher George Barna, after completing a two-year research project across America, has concluded, "Almost every church in our country has some type of discipleship program or set of activities; but stunningly few churches have a church of disciples."[7]

Why are so many churches across this country failing? We win people to Christ and they "sit, soak, and sour." I am appalled at the great number of believers who never grow up. Many who, supposedly, receive Christ as Savior never faithfully attend a Bible-believing church, and many of those who do take years before they grow to a moderate level of maturity. I agree with George Barna when he said, "the twenty-first century church has many 'followers' of Christ in the sense that I follow the Yankees: We dabble in Christianity. That's not what Jesus had in mind when he called us to be his disciples." He concludes by saying that "discipleship is not a program. It is not a ministry. It is a lifelong commitment to a lifestyle."[8] Why is there so little growth of so many people? According to Robert Coleman, the church as a whole in North America is barely keeping pace with the increase in population. In Western Europe there is a steady decline.[9] Why the decline? Why so many just dabbling in Christianity? Why are there so many who are Christian in name only? I believe it is because they were never biblically discipled. We have omitted discipleship from the Great Commission.

For much of our history the church has responded to the wrong command. You would think the Great Commission is to make converts and baptize them into church membership. Jesus didn't say, "Go therefore and make church buildings" or "Go therefore and make converts." That's not what Jesus told us to do. The Great Commission is to make disciples.

7. Barna, *Disciples*, 20.

8. Ibid., 19.

9. Coleman, *Discipleship*, 99.

Due to the urgency of our place in history, God is taking extraordinary steps to aid us in accomplishing this Commission. In the past century, God has poured people into the cities of the world at an unprecedented rate. Missiologists tell us that the first five years a person lives in another country, other than his homeland, he is more receptive to the gospel than at any other time. God is bringing the world to our urban doorstep so we can win them to Jesus Christ and make disciples out of them.

WHAT IS DISCIPLESHIP?

The Greek word for disciple (mathaytás*)* is the general word for learner or apprentice and always implies being in relationship to a teacher. The word "disciple" occurs 269 times in the New Testament. "Christian" is found three times and the term "believers" only two times. The New Testament is a book *about* disciples, *by* disciples, and *for* disciples of Jesus Christ.

If the main word for believers in the New Testament is disciple, doesn't that mean that all believers are disciples of Jesus Christ? Addressing a national seminar of Southern Baptist leaders, George Gallup said, "We find there is very little difference in ethical behavior between churchgoers and those who are not active religiously. . . . The levels of lying, cheating, and stealing are remarkably similar in both groups."[10] Our Christian society is in bad shape. And yet, most who faithfully attend an evangelical church would call themselves followers or disciples of Jesus Christ.

Even though the Greek translation for disciple means learner, it appears that the usage in the New Testament meant more than just a learner. According to Michael Wilkins in his book *Following the Master, A Biblical Theology of Discipleship*, "In most common usage, whether in the Roman or Greek world, a 'disciple' was a person who was committed to a significant master."[11] He goes on to say, "A disciple of Jesus during his earthly ministry was one who made a life commitment to him. . . . In a specific sense, a disciple of Jesus is one who has come to Jesus for eternal life, has claimed Jesus as Savior and God, and has embarked upon a life of following Jesus."[12] Discipleship, then, is the continuing process of

10. Gallup, *Leadership*, 17.
11. Wilkin, *Master*, 38.
12. Ibid., 39, 40.

growing as a disciple. Discipling another person is the process of helping another disciple grow to become like Jesus.

To understand the expectations placed upon the disciple-maker, we only need to read what Jesus states in the Gospel of Luke. Jesus sets very stringent requirements for all who would be his disciples. Jesus states three absolute requirements one must strive for, or he will not be included as a disciple of Jesus Christ.

First, he told his followers that one must deny self. In Luke 9:23, Jesus said, "If anyone wishes to come after Me, he must deny himself, and take up his cross daily and follow Me." Albert Barnes, in his commentary *Barnes' Notes*, says that to deny self means to "let him surrender to God his will, his affections, his body, and his soul. Let him not seek his own happiness as the supreme object, but be willing to renounce all, and lay down his life also, if required."[13]

In this passage Jesus also tells his listeners to take up their cross. Taking up one's cross is referring to personal goals, desires, and dreams that are released in favor of the goals conforming to God's will, designed to build his kingdom. It is the cross of self-sacrifice and self-denial, and we are to take it up on a daily basis. In Romans 12:1, the Apostle Paul says, "Therefore I urge you, brethren, by the mercies of God, to present your bodies a living and holy sacrifice, acceptable to God, which is your spiritual service of worship." He does not even consider this a major sacrifice, just our "spiritual service of worship" or, as the King James Version puts it, "your reasonable service."

Second, in Luke 14:26–27, Jesus implies that he must be placed as the absolute first priority in our lives. Jesus said, "If anyone comes to Me, and does not hate his own father and mother and wife and children and brothers and sisters, yes, and even his own life, he cannot be My disciple. Whoever does not carry his own cross and come after Me cannot be My disciple."

The word "hate" in Luke 14 is what scholars call a Semitic hyperbole—an obvious exaggeration designed to emphasize a thought. Our love for Christ should be so complete and wholehearted that, by comparison, the love for our family members and life itself would pale. Jesus will not be relegated to second or third place in our affection and devotion.

Third, a final requirement was made for those who would be his followers in Luke 14:28–33. Using two illustrations, Jesus taught that be-

13. Barnes, *Notes,* Matt 16:24–28.

ing a disciple includes commitment and sacrifice. The first illustration concerned the building of a tower (v. 28–30). Before a person begins to build, he should be sure he will be able to pay the full cost of the project. "For which one of you, when he wants to build a tower, does not first sit down and calculate the cost to see if he has enough to complete it?"

In order to press this point further, Jesus said in verse 33, "So then, none of you can be My disciple who does not give up all his own possessions." Jesus requires commitment and sacrifice of those who would be his disciples.

Jesus goes on by sharing another illustration, this time about a king who went out to battle (Luke 14:31–33). A king should be willing to sacrifice a desired victory and agree to a peace treaty if he concludes that his army is unable to defeat the enemy. Once again, Jesus is saying that we need to evaluate our commitment; we need to count the cost because we must be willing to give up everything for Jesus if we want to follow him. The people who were following Jesus throughout the countryside of Israel had done that. They had given up possessions and employment, knowing that the message Jesus was proclaiming was the most important thing on earth.

Jesus proclaimed that salt is good only as long as it contains the characteristics of saltiness as a climax to the teaching of his requirements to be a disciple in Luke 14:34–35. If it loses its saltiness, it has no value at all and is thrown out. This is true of a disciple. He must retain the seasoned character God requires. This salty character of being fully committed to Jesus Christ is not present in the lives of most Christians in the twenty-first century. They have not met the requirements and therefore are not his disciples. Therefore, in order to follow the Great Commission of Matthew 28, we need to help people grow to maturity. We need to guide the discipleship process especially during the early stages when the young disciple is hungry and motivated.

Dawson Trotman, the founder of The Navigators, called discipleship "Spiritual Pediatrics." I like the working definition provided by Allen Hadidian in his book *Successful Discipling* where he says, "Discipling others is the process by which a Christian, with a life worth emulating, commits himself for an extended period of time to a few individuals who have been won to Christ, the purpose being to aid and guide their growth to maturity and equip them to reproduce themselves in a third spiritual generation."[14]

14. Hadidian, *Discipling*, 31.

In addition to the definition above, Allen Hadidian suggests five ingredients of successful discipleship: First, he says the disciple-maker must have a life worth emulating. You may be wondering, what the qualifications are for one to be a disciple-maker. One of the primary requirements to be a discipler of other people is to have a life others can imitate. A godly role model is especially important in urban discipleship because of the lack of a Christian role model and a godly Father image. Having a life worth imitating doesn't mean we are sinless but that we are living a consistent Christian life. When we sin we are quick to confess it to God and correct our offense with the one we offended. We should not give the impression of perfection; nor should anyone put us on a pedestal, but they should be able to follow our example. Paul said in 1 Timothy 4:12, "Let no one look down on your youthfulness, but rather in speech, conduct, love, faith, and purity, show yourself an example of those who believe." (See also 2 Thess 3:9 and Heb 13:7.)

Second, in discipleship we commit ourselves for an extended period of time. We live in a fast-food society, but with discipleship there are no shortcuts. There are no crash courses because it is all about transformation, helping the person to grow spiritually. The length of time required to disciple another person depends on the person being discipled, on the spiritual maturity of the disciple, the number and type of strongholds that need to be conquered, and his level of commitment and motivation. In my experience, it will take a motivated man from one to one-and-a-half years of weekly ministry in his life for him to have a reasonably mature level of growth. When dealing with a person who is raised in a dysfunctional home, it often takes longer, sometimes from five to seven years.Third, for most effective one-on-one discipleship we need to commit ourselves to a few individuals. The temptation is to turn our discipleship into a class, thereby ministering to a larger group. Investing our lives in a few people seems risky, but when we change to a least effective larger class structure our effectiveness deteriorates. I am not implying that God can't and won't use us as we teach a group of people, but to have maximum impact in the lives of the individuals we are discipling, it is critically important that we limit our selection to a few people. This expands the impact of our relationship on other people, it makes it possible for them to see our example; we are able to hold our disciple accountable, and the opportunity to counsel, reproof, and correct our disciple is far more effective.

Fourth, the purpose is to guide the disciple to maturity. The mistake many make is to conduct a short series or study. I repeat what I said before: it takes time to grow. With discipleship, we commit ourselves to helping the person grow to a significant level of maturity, and that is laborious and time-consuming.

Fifth, Allen Hadidian said that in discipleship we equip the disciple to reproduce themselves in a third spiritual generation. Without reproduction, a species will cease to exist; so it is with spiritual reproduction. Fortunately, reproduction has never stopped; otherwise Christianity would have long ago expired. But imagine if the church had embarked on a ministry of discipleship with every new believer who desired to grow. Helping the hungry believer in the way described in this definition would result in the disciple sharing his faith, reproducing himself, and not ending his work with his new believer at the new convert stage, but going on to disciple and train him to share his faith and disciple others as well. Imagine the multiplication of mature believers the world would see if this took place. Imagine this impact of salt and light upon society.

Discipleship is often confused with mentoring. Aren't mentoring and discipleship basically the same thing? Yes, in that mentoring and discipleship seek to impart wisdom to an immature person. Both mentoring and discipleship do that. As Biehl says, "Mentoring is making available the mentor's personal strengths, resources, and network (friendships/contacts) to help a protégé reach his or her goals."[15] However, if we compare this definition with the definition of discipleship, we will see that we are talking about two different things. Discipleship deals especially with helping the person grow to a level of spiritual maturity; it is rooted in biblical wisdom, whereas mentoring may or may not be. Mentoring is more secular and has more to do with skill development. For example, one may mentor a person in an occupation or a position. We may mentor a person to be a good father or husband. After I have finished formal discipleship with a person, I often continue for a while in a mentoring relationship. I may mentor him to be a better husband or father. I often mentor him to be an effective disciple-maker. There is certainly some overlap between discipling and mentoring; however, for the young or immature believer I am convinced a concentrated discipleship ministry is most productive.

15. Biehl, *Mentoring*, 1.

One may ask if there are different methods available to use in the process of discipleship. I believe there are three types of discipleship that may be practiced: discipleship from a remote location, through small groups, and one-on-one discipleship.

Remote discipleship. Many may be surprised that I suggest one may disciple another person from faraway. For sure, this method would be the least effective, but I believe, used properly, it is nevertheless a form of discipleship. Just as in witnessing, the most effective approach is the method that is the most personal. For example, a personal letter would usually be more effective than a formal letter. A phone call may be more effective than a personal letter, and a face-to-face witness would usually be more effective than a phone call. Today, with all the technological advantages we have, we can send a letter through the postal system in a few days, instantly by e-mail, or, better yet, make a telephone call. When we lead someone to Christ who does not live a comfortable distance from our home, we assume that God, somehow, has let us off the hook and has absolved us of our responsibility.

Some of the New Testament books were written to an entire church, while many were written to individuals. Each book was then circulated to various small congregations meeting in homes. Luke wrote the Gospel of Luke and Acts to his friend Theophilus. Paul wrote some of his letters to encourage and instruct young believers. He wrote two letters to Timothy, a young pastor whom he had personally discipled. These two letters were a continuation of that discipleship process. Remote discipleship, whether it is through the postal service, email, or a telephone, is an important, and in many circumstances, the only way to disciple new believers in the military, those in prison, as well as others you lead to Christ that do not live near you.

One of the men I discipled had the opportunity to lead his mother and sister-in-law to Christ. He understood the principle that, as a spiritual father, he carried personal responsibility to help them grow and, at least, carried the responsibility to help them become grounded in the Christian faith. He challenged them both to enter into a discipleship relationship with him on Saturday mornings over the telephone. He mailed them lesson material for new believers and they agreed to complete one lesson each week. On Saturday morning, he would call his mother long distance and for about an hour lead a discussion about the basic growth concepts over the phone. He then hung up and called his sister-in-law and spent another hour with her. He continued this for thirteen weeks guiding them through the basic new Christian material. One day he shared his joy that his sister-in-law was serving as a leader in Vacation Bible School. She was excited to share that she was memorizing the Scripture verses right along with the children.

But you say, isn't that time consuming? I would answer yes! Isn't it expensive? I would say it could be! It's not convenient or easy to be a disciple of Jesus Christ, but responsibility comes with the privilege. My friend, for instance, was struggling to pay his way through a private college and yet, with God's strength, he found a way to begin initial discipleship with the two people he had led to Christ around that time, even though they did not live close to him. After all, can't we trust God for the financial burden? Often, I'm afraid, the real deterrent most likely comes down to priority and commitment.

Along with those who live far away, remote discipleship is also effective with those who are in prison and in the military. You may be positioned by God to have an impact in the lives of people like this. We must not avoid such a great opportunity.

Small groups. This second type of discipleship was one of the methods Jesus used. Imagine having only a brief time to live with the mission of providing salvation for all mankind and starting a movement that would affect millions of people for all eternity. The millions who never hear the truth would go into eternity without God. What method would you use? Christ chose to use small groups and life-on-life (sometimes one-on-one, one-on-two, or one-on-three) discipleship. He lived with his twelve disciples whom he constantly taught through instruction, correction, rebuke, personal example, and training.

Just having a Bible study does not insure discipleship. Small group discipleship must have well thought out content leading those who are growing disciples in a topical Bible study proceeding through material that would systematically aid their growth. The new believer needs basic instruction that the Bible calls "milk" before he is introduced to "meat." Hebrews 5:12–14 says, "For though by this time you ought to be teachers, you have need again for someone to teach you the elementary principles of the oracles of God, and you have come to need milk and not solid food. For everyone who partakes only of milk is not accustomed to the word of righteousness, for he is an infant. But solid food is for the mature who, because of practice, have their senses trained to discern good and evil." I believe this is why many new believers never grow or they grow very slowly. We just invite them to church and, if they come at all, they get a few chunks of meat that they cannot spiritually digest. When they get milk, the teaching is inconsistent and non-progressive. It is not the type of milk needed for their level of development and therefore does not bring effective growth.

Among the advantages of small group discipleship are the close fellowship and camaraderie that comes from a small group, enabling people to really get to know each other. The dynamic of close friendships can be developed where positive peer influence and encouragement helps the Christian life to flourish. These types of groups provide an emotional home where the believer can feel accepted, providing an atmosphere for spiritual development. Small group interaction encourages the members and exposes them to God's personal working in their lives. A well-planned small group Bible study is also a very effective way to teach biblical truth through both instruction and interaction.

An effective small group discipleship ministry should include several elements. First, each member should sign a covenant or commitment to the program agreeing to attend every meeting except excused absences such as sickness or a few weeks of vacation. The commitment also includes an agreement to complete all assignments before the meeting. Second, it is very important to set up a system of accountability. Encourage each one to choose another person in the group as their weekly accountability partner. If the small group includes both men and women, accountability partners should be the same gender and one's accountability partner should be someone other than his or her spouse. Third, this is not just a Bible study. The curriculum should be carefully chosen for growth, depending on the level of maturity of the group. One group could be a new believers class going through foundational principles. A second type of group could be an intermediate class covering basic Bible doctrine and other Christian living materials. Additional classes could be more advanced.

One-on-one discipleship. The third and most effective form of discipleship is the one-on-one approach. The great advantage of this type of discipleship is the impact a relationship can have in helping a person make a transformation in their Christian life. The personal example of the discipler in this relationship becomes a major factor along with the natural accountability. This approach enables the disciple-maker to have an in-depth knowledge of where the disciple is in his growth, which leads to biblical counseling, exhorting, advising, rebuking, correcting, teaching, and guiding. This highly personal form of discipleship enables the leader to pace the process congruent to the needs of the disciple. It does not require much forethought to realize how each of these advantages makes one-on-one discipleship very effective and needed in urban ministry, especially in the inner city.

To further understand what is meant by discipleship, let me make five additional observations. First, I do not do the discipling. Who is the discipler? Of course, the Holy Spirit is the discipler using me as a channel and a living example. Second, they are not my disciples. They are being discipled to follow Jesus Christ. Third, discipleship is a team ministry. Many people will be involved in the process: the pastor of the church, the primary disciple-maker, his Sunday Bible study teacher, and so on. God will use each of these people as part of the discipleship process. A wise discipler will use the available people and resources to best accomplish his purpose. Fourth, one person must assume the responsibility; here is where we have failed through the centuries. If no one assumes the responsibility, we have immediately degenerated to a traditional model of just inviting new converts to our programs. A primary person with whom there can be a significant relationship, along with an accountability structure, must be central to all effective discipleship. Fifth, discipleship is a command, not an option; discipleship is our Great Commission.

Now that we have outlined God's *purpose* for this age, *to build his church*, and God's *plan* for the church, to *make disciples*, we will devote the next chapter to God's *procedure* to accomplish his plan.

REVIEW QUESTIONS

1. What is God's *purpose* and *plan*, as described in this chapter?
2. According to Michael Wilkins, what is his specific definition of discipleship?
3. What are the three requirements Jesus gave his followers and that one must strive for if he is to be a disciple of Christ?
4. According to Allen Hadidian's working definition of discipleship, what are the five ingredients of successful discipleship?
5. What are the three types of discipleship listed by the author?

6

Turn the World Upside Down

Great Impact Multiplied

THE STORY OF THE first-century church is a story of the miracle of how a totally ill-equipped church (by our standards) "turned the world upside down" (Acts 17:6 ESV). We are talking about a people with no technological assets. They had no television, Internet, computers, cell phones, or air or ground transportation that was faster than walking. They had no printing capabilities, no loud speakers, and none of the Bible research tools we so heavily depend on as we prepare sermons and lessons. They didn't even have much, if any, of the New Testament available for church use; yet aided by a willing heart and the power of the Holy Spirit, they "turned the world upside down." How did they do it? Why was their influence so dynamic and so revolutionary? In two thousand years the church has never even come close to matching their impact. What was their secret?

In the previous chapter, we calibrated our compass by getting our direction adjusted. We discussed "God's Purpose for this Age" and "God's Plan for the Church." Now in this chapter, as we explore the reason for the great success of the early church, let's consider the *procedure* God wants us to follow.

GOD'S PROCEDURE FOR ACCOMPLISHING HIS PLAN

There is a modern fable in which a father told his two sons that he had a gift for each. To one, he would give a dollar each week for fifty-two weeks. To the other son, his first week's gift would be one cent, just a penny, but each week thereafter he would multiply the total accumulated to date by two. Well, when given a chance to choose, the older son quickly chose a dollar a week because in one year he would have fifty-two dollars. The younger son, having to yield to the older, reluctantly accepted the leftover option. Of course, a review of exponential growth quickly shows that the son given the pennies, multiplied each week, would greatly pass up the son with the dollar added each week. Chart number three illustrates the value of multiplication over addition. When we multiply by two the growth begins slowly; in fact, it takes twelve weeks (or rounds of multiplication by two) for the younger son starting with one cent to pass up the boy who received one dollar each week. Notice on the chart how multiplication begins to expand. By the fifty-second week, repeatedly multiplying the running total contribution by two, the younger son had $22,517,998,136,852.50 (over 22 and a half trillion dollars.) Simple multiplication as described begins very slowly but has tremendous exponential power.

COMPARING ADDITION WITH MULTIPLICATION

Week	Add	Multiply By Two
1	$1.00	$0.01
2	2.00	0.02
3	3.00	0.04
4	4.00	0.08
5	5.00	0.16
6	6.00	0.32
7	7.00	0.64
8	8.00	1.28
9	9.00	2.56
10	10.00	5.12
20	20.00	5,242.88
30	30.00	5,368,709.12
40	40.00	5,497,558,138.88
50	50.00	5,629,499,534,213.12
51	51.00	11,258,999,068,426.20
52	$52.00	$22,517,998,136,852.50

God's *procedure* to accomplish his *plan* involves the principal of multiplication. Multiplication is a fundamental principle of life. In Genesis 1:28, God said to Adam and Eve, "Be fruitful and multiply, and fill the earth." If God had used the addition method, the population of the earth would have only included Adam, Eve, and their children. Even the method God uses in the reproduction process is by multiplication. The embryo, once fertilized, begins multiplying by two beginning very slowly and gradually accelerating to an explosive degree. Even after four or five months of pregnancy, a mother shows little visible growth; however, in the last few months of pregnancy one can see major changes because of the unparalleled growth of the child.

Multiplication is also God's method of spiritual reproduction as seen in God's Word. The supreme example is the life of Jesus, who came to earth to provide redemption for mankind. He only had three years of ministry available to begin a movement—recruiting, discipling, and training his followers whom he would use to change the course of history. Jesus chose a multiplication method beginning with twelve men whom he poured his life into. They had the mission to not only win others to Christ (addition) but to make disciples in every nation (multiplication) (Matt 28:19–20). Jesus clearly desired for his disciples to multiply themselves. He not only prayed for his disciples but, in John 17:20–26, he prayed for those his disciples would reach.

By the sixth chapter of Acts, addition changed to multiplication as "[t]he word of God increased; and the number of the disciples multiplied in Jerusalem greatly" (Acts 6:7 KJV). One of the followers of Christ we read about in the book of Acts is Philip, who was directed to the Ethiopian Eunuch. The Eunuch believed in Christ and went back to Ethiopia (Acts 8:26–39). According to tradition, the entire nation and the surrounding country were won to Christ. Note the four generations of multiplication:

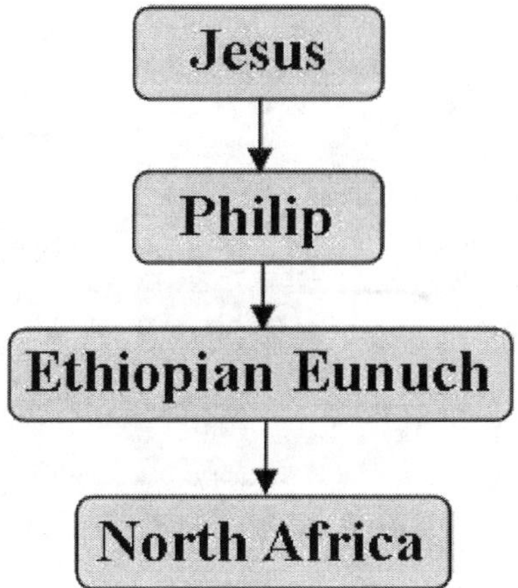

Through the life of Paul, Silvanus, and Timothy, we see the example of reaching the Thessalonians who in turn reached people in Macedonia and Achaia (Acts 16:9–12; 19:22; 20:1–2; Rom 15:26; 1 Thess 1:1). Paul told Timothy, "The things which you have heard from me in the presence of many witnesses, entrust these to faithful men who will be able to teach others also" (2 Tim 2:2). In the next two graphics, we see the ministry of Jesus through Paul multiplied to five generations.

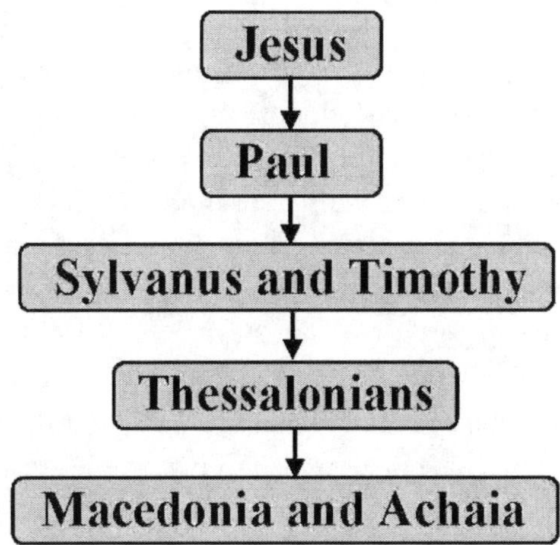

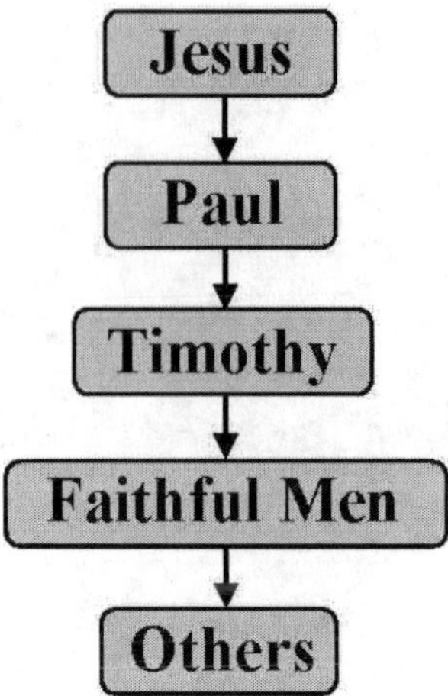

Extending from a few hundred believers, the Christian community within three decades had multiplied four hundred fold, which represents an annual increase of 22 percent. As stated earlier, by the beginning of the fourth century, when Constantine was allegedly converted to Christianity, the number of disciples may have reached ten or twelve million, or roughly a tenth of the total population of the Roman Empire.[1] This kind of growth doesn't come by just adding new converts or the transfer of membership from one church to another; it comes by multiplication.[2]

After the beginning of the fourth century, discipleship multiplication, as described above, was seldom emphasized. However, there were two men living at the same time in history who had a great impact for God but who were using very different methods. These two contemporaries, George Whitefield and John Wesley, were both men used by God to awaken revival and touch two continents in the eighteenth century.

Whitefield compared his ministry with Wesley's and confessed, "my brother Wesley acted wisely. The souls that were awakened under his ministry he joined in class [small groups], and thus preserved the fruits of his labors. This I neglected, and my people are a rope of sand."[3] Whitefield's ministry spawned many thousands of converts to Christ, but in terms of lasting impact, he saw little fruit. His converts were like

1. Schaff, *History,* 198.
2. Coleman, *Discipleship*, 30.
3. Jackson, *Methodism*, 69.

a rope of sand because he didn't make disciples. Wesley, on the other hand, left behind a movement with such increasing momentum that the generations after his death saw more disciples and churches planted than he saw during his lifetime. Why was John Wesley so successful? He was successful because he set up a system of methods allowing ordinary people to do extraordinary things, a system of discipleship.

In John Wesley's system, small groups were organized that met weekly with four to six members each. The members had to have a high commitment to the group, which included strong accountability. His system had three types of groups: one for seekers called Classes, a second designed for Christian growth he called Bands, and a third group called Select Societies was designed for personal holiness and discipleship among leaders. It's easy to see why Methodism grew far beyond its founder's lifetime and even exists today.

Imagine for a moment we had two modern-day disciples of Christ who developed their own strategies. The first man, having a great passion for the lost, decided that with God's help he would win one thousand people to Christ each and every day. The second man decided, with God's help, he would win one person to Christ but wouldn't stop there. He would spend a year discipling him as a follower of Jesus Christ. During that time he would so ingrain in him the importance of discipleship that after one year had passed, he and his disciple would split off and they both would win one person to Christ and disciple that person for one year. What would happen if both men continued this process? By the end of the first year the evangelist would have won 365,000 people to Christ, the disciple-maker would have won and discipled only one person (a total of two including himself.) On the chart below we can see the multiplication principle worked out comparing evangelism (addition) and discipleship (multiplication by two).

Comparison of Evangelism by Addition and Discipleship by Multiplication		
Years	Evangelist	Discipler
1	365,000	2
2	730,000	4
10	3,650,000	1,024
17	6,205,000	131,072
23	8,395,000	8,388,608
26	9,490,000	67,108,864
30	10,950,000	1,073,741,824
33	12,045,000	8,589,934,592

As you can see from the chart, it would take over twenty-three years for the discipler to catch up with the evangelist. But then notice the exponential growth. To reach the world for Christ it would take the evangelist, with an addition approach, 10,960 years, assuming no one was born and no one died. The discipler, using a discipleship multiplication model, would not only reach the world for Christ, but disciple the world of six billion people by the middle of the thirty-second year.

Converting the World of Six Billion by Addition Compared to Multiplication

One person winning 1,000 people each day (addition) would take 10,960 years to convert the entire world.

One person winning and discipling another person for one year, with each discipled person thereafter continuing the process, would take 32½ years to win and disciple the entire world.

I am not naive to the reality that the multiplication process will break down. Not everybody will receive Christ, disciplers and those being discipled will face problems, some will not persevere, and some will yield to satanic attack and drop out. Then, of course, there are those who will choose the wrong person to disciple. Whatever the reason, the process will break down. However, the impact on the world will be so much greater following a multiplication discipleship strategy. Jesus Christ and the disciples used a discipleship multiplication strategy, and it turned the world upside down. We are to follow their example.

Walter Henrichson said, "The reason that the Church of Jesus Christ finds it so difficult to stay on top of the Great Commission is that the population of the world is multiplying while the church is merely adding. Addition can never keep pace with multiplication."[4] Imagine what God would do through you if you were to prioritize your time so that you were continually leading people to Christ and discipling them, continuing this through your entire life. Imagine if each qualified church member would to do the same. What a great impact we would have on our city and our world for Christ! God's *procedure* to accomplish his *plan* of discipleship is *multiplication*.

I have a dream. A dream that someday in eternity there will be a great family tree of people who were discipled because God used me. No, they won't all be discipled by me directly; in fact, there will be many I won't even know. Most will be the spiritual descendents of those whom God used me to impact. My prayer is that God challenges you in the same way that he has me.

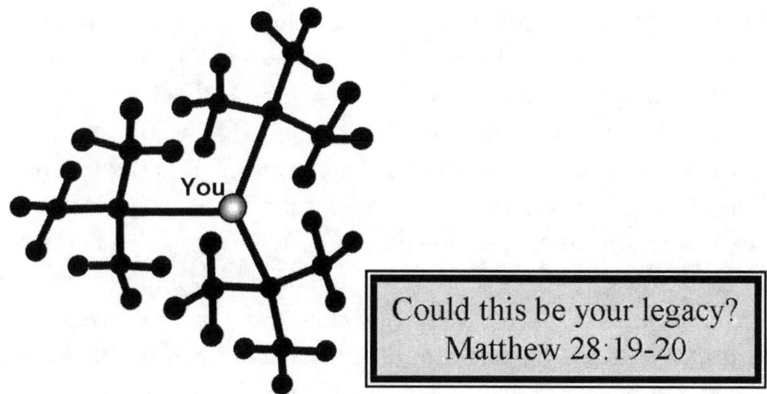

4. Henrichsen, *Disciples*, 142.

God's *purpose* for this age is to *build his church.*
God's *plan* for the church is to *make disciples.*
God's *procedure* to accomplish his plan is *multiplication.*

BASICS OF A DISCIPLESHIP MINISTRY

Christopher Adsit says that discipleship is like a three-legged stool. Each leg is indispensable for a stable discipleship ministry. The three pillars or legs of discipleship are relationship, content, and prayer.[5] If one of these legs is missing, the stool cannot stand. So it is with discipleship.

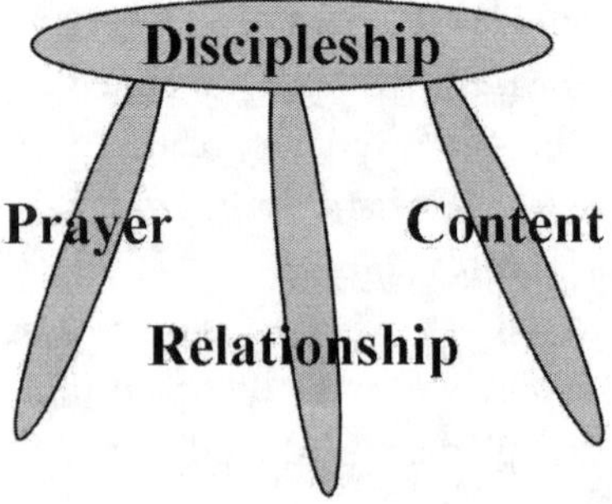

Relationship. Many so-called discipleship ministries are nothing but a course or a study series. The content may be strong but the process is lacking the leg of relationship. Relationship is critical because the disciple will learn far more from who we are than what we say. The old adage "more is caught than taught" is a fact of life. Disciples need to see the Christian life lived out, and he needs someone to follow. The relationship of the disciple-maker to the disciple affords the opportunity for correction, counsel, and accountability. Without the relationship element, we have drifted back to the traditional approach that has failed to produce the multiplying disciples we need to fulfill the Great Commission.

Content. If we have relationship without content, we have nothing more than a "friendship circle" or a "coffee clutch." There is no systematic approach to move the new believer on the growth continuum to matu-

5. Adsit, *Disciplemaking*, 54–55.

rity. In Matthew 28:20, Jesus said that part of the Great Commission is, "teaching them to observe all that I commanded you." He was talking about the necessity of education in the discipleship process. Information is never given for the sake of knowledge alone but for the transformation of our minds and lives.

Prayer. If prayer is missing, there will be no power and our discipleship will be ineffective. We cannot change the heart; only the Holy Spirit can do that. When we try to disciple in our own strength, we experience utter failure in terms of transformed lives. In John 15:5 Jesus said, "Apart from Me you can do nothing." Discipleship needs to be bathed in prayer, asking for God's direction, the Spirit's filling, and transformation for the one we are discipling.

Many programs and Bible studies referred to as discipleship ministries are lacking one of these legs. Each element of discipleship—*relationship*, *content*, and *prayer*—is necessary if we are to have effective and biblical discipleship.

SIX CHARACTERISTICS OF THE DISCIPLESHIP MINISTRY OF JESUS

One cannot think about the life of Christ without being intrigued by the moment in history at which he chose to come. He had no modern conveniences such as a cell phone, no automobile, or airplane. He had no publishing capabilities, no computer, Internet, television, amplifiers, or microphones. He had no church building or modern curriculum, not even the complete Word of God. He came in an era where the new movement would have to adjust from the Jewish economy of law to a new age of grace. Why didn't he come in a modern era? Why didn't he come in the twenty-first century with all the conveniences technology has to offer, with the best translations the world has ever seen? Christ came during the worst era in history and changed the world forever. After following Jesus for just a few years, his disciples turned the world upside down (Acts 17:6 ESV). They didn't do it using mass media or mass evangelism, but they did it through a few men. Jesus himself had only a thousand days to save all mankind and he chose to invest most of his limited time with only twelve.

As we observe the life of Jesus recorded in the gospels, I would like to note six qualities in his discipleship ministry that need to be incorporated in our lives as disciple-makers.

First, he had an intimate relationship with those he discipled. Jesus Christ placed a major emphasis on relationship. Mark 3:14 says, "He appointed twelve, so that they would be with him." Jesus not only lived with his disciples twenty-four hours a day, but he was a perfect model of how to live. Someone has said that 90 percent of discipleship is relationship. The disciples of Jesus were gradually transformed as they interacted with him, learned at his feet, and observed his life.

Listen to what Paul said about this important ingredient of relationship. "Having so fond an affection for you, we were well-pleased to impart to you not only the gospel of God but also our own lives, because you had become very dear to us" (1 Thess 2:8). Clearly, the Apostle Paul maintained a dynamic relationship with those he taught.

Discipleship through relationships is especially effective in the urban setting because the value system of urban people, with the exception of the upwardly mobile, puts much importance on relationships. In fact, relational discipleship is well received by poor people and people of many ethnic groups throughout the world.

Second, he practiced perfect guardianship. A guardian is one who has the responsibility for another. This includes providing protection, rescuing those who stray, praying, counseling, teaching, warning, and rebuking them when necessary. The word picture of a guardian in the New Testament is the shepherd watching over his sheep. Jesus, of course, is the Good Shepherd, and the believers are his sheep. When he went to heaven, he sent the Holy Spirit to continue this ministry. As the spiritual guardian, the discipler is overseeing the spiritual walk of the disciple. In Hebrews 13:17 we see this responsibility of guardianship that church leaders exercise where it says that one should "Obey your leaders and submit to them, for they keep watch over your souls as those who will give an account."

Third, his duration was until completion. It would be ridiculous for a farmer to cram farm work in like many students cram for a final exam. It would be absurd to procrastinate, planting in the spring, then playing all summer, and cramming in the fall to bring in the harvest. The farmer knows the price one must pay and the process that needs to be followed. In farming, one always reaps what he sows, and there are no shortcuts. So it is with discipleship—spiritual growth takes time. Jesus Christ only had three years, but he chose to invest the bulk of his time discipling a few chosen men. Paul began his discipleship ministry with Timothy around 53 AD. Fourteen years later he was still discipling Timothy as we see in the letter of 2 Timothy. I am not suggesting that anyone should continue discipling each person for fourteen years, but my point is that there are no shortcuts. We cannot conduct a six-week course and expect that we have adequately discipled people.

Many city dwellers have experienced an unstable life. One may not know his father, his mother has a temporary boyfriend, and they have moved from one apartment to the next. His entire experience is unstable; therefore, he desperately needs consistency and stability. There will not be solid growth in the lives of many urban people, especially those in the inner city, unless the discipler makes a commitment to stick with the disciple to completion.

A disciple-maker should persist with discipleship until he has completed the process or until someone else takes over. The length of time will vary from person to person depending on the motivation of the one being discipled. Generally speaking, discipleship will take a minimum of one year to bring a motivated adult to a significant level of maturity. As I said earlier, inner city people from dysfunctional homes will often take much longer, even as much as five to seven years. It has been said that it takes a hundred years to make a great oak tree, but only three months to grow a squash. We have grown far too many spiritual squashes. Our priority must be to develop people, with the aid of the Holy Spirit, into spiritually mature disciples of Jesus Christ.

Fourth, he prepared his disciples through teaching and training. Much has been written about Jesus, the master teacher. He continually taught through instruction, parables, and example. Jesus was a perfect model for the disciples to follow. In fact, as written by Robert Coleman, when it comes to his discipleship, Jesus was his own method.[6] Telling people what we mean is good, but it is far better to show them. People are looking for a demonstration not just an explanation.[7]

Jesus also trained his disciples by assigning them work. He sent the twelve out two-by-two (Mark 6:7–13) and sent the seventy-two disciples on a similar mission (Luke 10:1–11). I would suspect, though it is not explicitly noted in the Bible, that there was time given to debriefing. Likely, opportunity was given for testimonies, a report, discussion, evaluation, and instruction.

6. Coleman, *Evangelism*, 74.

7. Ibid., 76.

Fifth, he created the perfect environment. Environment is very important for the growth of a tender plant. If you plant a garden in the Mojave Desert, you wouldn't expect it to grow unless you constructed a hothouse where you could control the amount of sun, water, and heat. The environment for the new believer is just as important. If the new believer continues to hang out with unsaved friends, they will choke out his growth until they are weeded from his life. One Corinthians 15:33 says, "Bad company corrupts good morals." (See also Ps 1:1–3; Prov 13:20) After thirty-six years of discipling men and supervising discipleship ministries, I can't think of anything that more regularly prevents a new believer from becoming spiritually established. We can help him create a new environment by planting him in the church with the soft soil of Christian friendships: God's people who love the Lord. In this environment, rapid and healthy growth will follow.

What about retaining friendships with unsaved people for the purpose of witnessing? Of course one cannot divorce himself from the world. We are in the world but we must not be of the world. We should look for opportunities to be a witness to our unsaved friends and relatives. In fact, we should pray for them daily and plan opportunities where we can share our faith; however, the immature believer must not make the nonbeliever his source of fellowship, or spiritual development will be hindered. Environment is critical for healthy development, and the discipler should do all he can to encourage the proper balance.

Sixth, he provided focus through purposeful concentration. One of the reasons for the failure of the modern church is our obsession to minister to as many at a time as possible. This is important to note because the value of relationship mentioned above is diminished as the group size is increased. Concentration on a few is vitally important for effective discipleship. Jesus had various groups he concentrated on at different intensities. The smaller the group the more time he spent with them.

The Principle of Concentration in the Ministry of Jesus

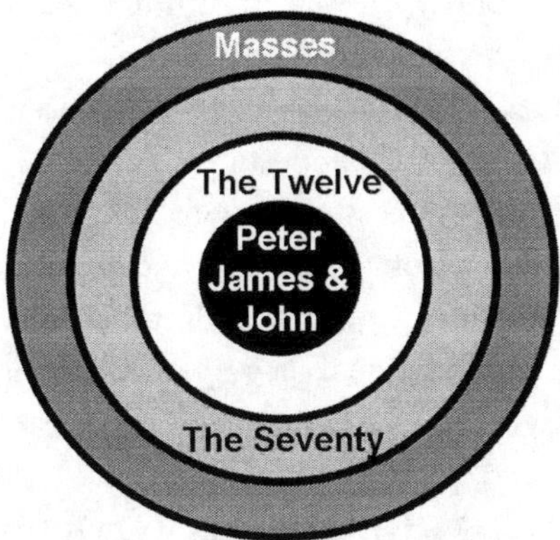

The masses came and went—some believed, most did not. They came for various reasons. Some came to be healed, others came for food, and many came to see what the commotion was all about. As with any large gathering, the purpose was very limited. Some of the masses believed and became followers of Jesus Christ; some were numbered among the seventy. Undoubtedly, many of these were among the one hundred and twenty present in the upper room on the Day of Pentecost. They were taught and, to some degree, trained as we can see when they were sent out two-by-two to preach the gospel (Luke 10:1–11).

His ministry to the seventy was much more concentrated than his ministry to the masses. His ministry to the twelve was much more concentrated than to the seventy. He lived with the twelve, having an intimate relationship with them day and night. They not only heard his teaching but they asked many questions, most of which were never recorded in the gospels. Jesus' greatest teaching tool in discipling the twelve was his living example.

Finally, there was the one-on-one ministry or often, in the ministry of Christ, one-on-three with Peter, James, and John. He took them with him to the sick room of Jairus's daughter (Matt 9:23–26; Mark 5:35–43Mark 5:35–43; Luke 8:49–56). They went with him to the Mount of Transfiguration (Matt 17:1; Mark 9:2; Luke 9:28). Peter, James, and John also went on ahead with Jesus when he asked them to watch and pray while he prayed alone at Gethsemane just before his betrayal (Matt

26:36–46; Mark 14:32–42; Luke 22:39–46). It is a wonderful gift that we can read of the many instances in which Christ spoke to these three men giving them instruction, encouragement, and sometimes a rebuke, and at the same time, providing a perfect example for them to emulate. As we analyze the work of Christ, we can summarize the last three years of his life as a ministry of concentration.

Concentration is critical to any effective discipleship ministry. Waylan Moore in *New Testament Follow-up* states, "A decision that our ministry will be intensive, rather than extensive will change our whole life. Quality begets quantity. It takes vision to train one man to reach the mass."[8] A wise decision for any servant of God is spending his life with the priority of concentrating on a few individuals at a time. Following this methodology over the long haul will produce eternal fruit and great joy.

HOW TO CHOOSE ONE TO DISCIPLE

Since we are going to devote a concentrated amount of time with a few individuals, it is important we are selective as to who we disciple as well as the number.

How many should one disciple at a time? For most laypeople, the maximum number of people a person will be able to handle is one or two. If you are as fortunate as I am, as a Pastor of Discipleship, to be able to include some discipleship in your daily schedule, you may be able to handle more. However, it is still better to concentrate on a few individuals. Effective discipleship includes more than just meeting once a week for a Bible study. One should always look for opportunities to spend time with the disciple beyond the Bible study. I often take men with me to visit at the jail, hospital, nursing home, on home visitation, out to lunch, and have them over to my home. This provides an opportunity to minister through relationship and example. Like the Marines, let us look "for a few good men" or women.

They should be God-given people. There are many people that may appear needful and desirous of discipleship. Those serving in pastoral positions will find many people that would love to be discipled by one with pastoral training and experience. It is important to be reminded we only have one life to disciple people and therefore a limited number of people to impact. That's why we need to be selective with whom we

8. Moore, *Follow-up*, 68.

invest our time. Jesus referred to his followers in John 17:6 as men God gave him to disciple. He taught them and spent considerable time praying for them (John 17:6–10). God wants to give men or women to us for the same purpose. We must ask ourselves if we are praying that God will reveal to us those God-given people?

They should not be chosen hastily. Jesus took one-and-a-half years to choose his twelve disciples. He did not rush because he knew what was at stake. I'm not suggesting that it will take one-and-a-half years or more to choose someone to disciple, but we should not be hasty. Get acquainted with the prospect, observe his character, evaluating if he meets the "*Father*" criteria explained below, at least to some degree. If you believe he fulfills the criteria, meet with him and explain the commitment required. He needs to see the importance, just as you do; once he does, he will be eager to agree to the commitment.

Prayer is essential in selecting one to disciple. In Luke 6, we notice that Christ had people who had been following him. According to verse 12 and 13, Jesus spent a whole night in prayer and then chose his twelve disciples from among the larger group of followers. Knowing that the Son of God thought it necessary to spend such time in prayer before he chose those he would disciple magnifies how we need to put much more emphasis on prayer, seeking God's direction before we select the one we will disciple. As I said before, we have only one life to spend for God. It is eternally important that we follow God's direction from selection through completion. Jesus said, "for apart from me you can do nothing" (John 15:5; Matt 6:33). Therefore, prayer is essential.

The prospect's ability should not be a factor in your decision. We must be careful not to pick one to disciple because of their talent, intelligence, gifts, pleasing personality, or outgoing nature. If we were going to select disciples for Jesus, understanding their background and training, we probably would not have selected any of the twelve. Concerning these men, Robert Coleman noted, "They do not impress us as being key men. None of them occupied prominent places in the synagogue nor did any of them belong to the Levitical priesthood. For the most part they were common laboring men, probably having no professional training beyond the rudiments of knowledge necessary for their vocation."[9] Jesus did not base his selection on the abilities of the prospects. Rather, he

9. Coleman, *Evangelism*, 28.

selected them based on what they could become. Therefore, it becomes critical that the people we choose to disciple are given to us by God.

The gender of the disciple you choose is critical. Even though it may be obvious, the importance of discipling someone of the same gender is a standard that many have mistakenly violated. Discipling others is a long-term process that becomes both intensive and intimate. Therefore, attempting to disciple someone of the opposite sex is both ineffective and dangerous. The discipleship process includes informal counseling that is often personal and gender sensitive. A wise disciple-maker does not enter this type of relationship with one of the opposite sex. I am often asked if it is okay to disciple one's spouse. Of course, the intimate and sensitive aspects would be no problem in such a case. However, because of the accountability and authority the disciple-maker has over his disciple, it is best that someone other than a spouse conduct the discipleship. Also, a person of the same gender can more fully understand the problems and needs of another of the same sex and can address these needs better. I am not implying that the husband should not have spiritual input and responsibility regarding his wife but, rather, the intensive relationship of discipleship is better suited with another of the same gender.

Certain qualities should exist in the prospect. As I stated before, it is vitally important that we prayerfully and carefully select the people we disciple. Certain qualities should exist before entering a deep relationship beyond the new Christian phase. A young believer will not be advanced in any or all of these traits, but I believe we should see a degree of these qualities in him, assuring us that spending the kind of time necessary to disciple that person will be well spent. The person who enters an in-depth program of discipleship with others becomes a "spiritual father" (or mother) to them. Therefore, we should look and pray for the six qualities enumerated by the acronym *F a t h e r*.

***F**aithful*: In 2 Timothy 2:2, Paul instructed the young pastor Timothy by saying: "The things which you have heard from me in the presence of many witnesses, entrust these to faithful men who will be able to teach others also." Notice it didn't say *slothful men*. Paul is concerned that the time Timothy spends in discipleship is not squandered away in a discipleship relationship that is not effective. When selecting someone to disciple, look for wheat not chaff. I have been in discipleship relationships where the disciple is characterized by chaff. He will do nothing but drain you physically, emotionally, and spiritually. The disciples of Christ were called followers. They followed Christ; he never chased them.

Ask these questions: Is he or she coming to church with some consistency? Has the person demonstrated some faithfulness in the new-Christians class? What do others say about him? Have you observed his life? Ask God to reveal to you whether or not he is faithful.

During the first appointment, I always lay out the requirements I expect from the one I disciple. I explain that God is going to do great things to develop his spiritual growth. If we enter this relationship, God will be giving me spiritual oversight and authority over him. To see the kind of growth God wants to give, there are certain requirements. Then I list my expectations which include: regular attendance in the services of the church, never missing a scheduled meeting with me unless approved, always being on time at meetings, and completing all assignments on time. I also emphasize the importance of contacting me by phone or text in the event that he will not be able to make a meeting with me or if he will be late. I usually put this in a written form as a covenant he signs. Faithfulness is a primary characteristic and must not be overlooked.

A*vailable*: He may have all the other qualities you are looking for, but if he doesn't have the time to meet, obviously, he cannot be discipled effectively by you. It may not be an issue of commitment, but perhaps your schedule and the prospective disciple's are in conflict. The answer may be to find someone else to disciple him or wait until God makes it possible.

T*eachable*: Does he have a genuine desire to learn? Is there a willingness to submit to being taught? Does he ask questions, or does he just want to debate issues? This eagerness will be displayed as he shows up for other learning opportunities such as Bible studies and services of the church. During your meeting with him, he should be alert and engaged, sometimes taking notes and often asking questions. You should quickly pick up that he has a keen desire to learn about God and to effectively live the Christian life.

I met with a man once who was constantly trying to change my mind on issues, putting me on the defensive. When I tried to instruct him, he would change the subject because he was not interested in being taught. He just wanted to display his knowledge. The joy of discipling another comes when your disciple is eager to learn. It seems like he can't get enough and has come to you so you will help him grow. To be teachable is a quality that will bring much joy to you as you watch your disciple grow.

***H**eart for God*: Does he have a desire to know God? In Matthew 22:37–38, Jesus said, "You shall love the Lord your God with all your heart, and with all your soul, and with all your mind." Of course, we will fall short of this command, but if a person desires to be a disciple of Jesus Christ, he must have a desire to know him. Jesus also said, "If anyone wishes to come after Me, he must deny himself, and take up his cross daily and follow Me" (Luke 9:23). This command will only be followed by one who has a heart for God.

***E**ager to Serve*: I don't know of anything outside of God's Word and the active work of the Holy Spirit in one's life that more fully motivates us than the involvement of service to the Lord. A great sense of gratification comes in knowing you are doing something that is bigger than you and of eternal value. The sense that the Holy Spirit is using you to impact another person's life is thrilling indeed.

Jimmy was a nineteen-year-old homeless young man and a new believer in Jesus Christ. He came to our city to move in with his brother who lived at a nearby military base. When I found he would not be allowed to live on the base, we took him into our home, and what I thought would be a few days lasted a year. During that time, I fathered and discipled him.

Jimmy had developed a high level of proficiency in the martial art of Kung Fu, which I used in several programs as a tool to draw kids. That summer we took Jimmy with us on a youth mission trip to Casa Grande, Arizona, to work with the children of Mexican migrant workers. One day at our children's club we encouraged the kids to bring their friends the next day to see the Kung Fu expert. The word spread rapidly, drawing a large number of children as visitors. Jimmy put on a Kung Fu demonstration, breaking pieces of wood and a stack of cement capping stones. The demonstration was followed by his testimony of how he received Jesus Christ as his personal Savior and how God had changed his life. His witness had a great impact on the children that day and a number of kids received Christ.

When I noticed there were six teenagers in the crowd of children, I asked Jimmy to take them to a back room while we continued the children's program. I asked him to share more about how he got into this sport and about his workout regiment. I told him to tell them more about how God helped him each day and what Jesus meant to him. Since we had not planned for this situation, Jimmy was afraid he would not know what to say. I told him that God would give him the words to say. Jimmy took the boys to the back room as he was instructed and shared about his sport and his relationship with Jesus Christ.

After the meeting, Jimmy eagerly told me how God worked through him, and as he talked to the boys he saw tears running down the cheeks of several of them. I asked Jimmy if God helped him as I said he would. He told me it was amazing, and that he thought of things he forgot he knew, and he shared verses he didn't know he remembered. Jimmy said he felt like he grew six inches spiritually that day. This experience was the highlight of the trip for this young man and probably the high point in his Christian life since salvation. Serving God has a profound impact on our motivation to love and serve him even more.

***R**espect for Authority*: With this term, I am referring to the importance of respecting the authority of the one who has physical and spiritual oversight over the disciple. In the city, there is a common disrespect for government officials, especially the police. Often there is a resistance to anyone exercising authority and holding one accountable for his actions. Romans 13:1–2 says, "Every person is to be in subjection to the governing authorities. . . . Therefore whoever resists authority has opposed the ordinance of God, and they who have opposed will receive condemnation upon themselves." If the individual doesn't respect the civil authorities, he will likely disrespect your authority as a leader and it will be difficult to disciple him. A general disrespect for authority will result in disrespect for God's authority as well.

How do I discern if the prospective disciple has the *Father* qualifications? We discern this by prayer and simple observation. If he is a new believer he should begin attending a new-Christian class either in a small group or with another person one-on-one. Has he been faithful to this series? Has he done his assignments? Does he memorize the assigned verses? If there are no organized classes, begin taking him through the new-Christian materials one-on-one with no commitment beyond this stage. Once the series is completed, you will be ready to judge if he meets the criteria. If the prospective disciple doesn't have these qualities, at least to a degree, it may not be wise to invest massive time beyond new-Christian classes. As you spend time praying, asking God to reveal his God-given person to you, he will lead you in your decision.

An equally important question is: am I qualified to be a discipler? To be an effective "spiritual father" (or mother), we must have the *Father* qualities ourselves. If we are lacking in one or more of these qualities, we must ask God to develop us in these areas and to help us to make an aggressive effort to add these qualities to our walk. We cannot be discouraged from the great calling and mandate to make disciples. You might be thinking, "Is there hope for the kind of growth in my life that will enable me to demonstrate the qualities needed to be an effective disciple-maker?" Paul, under the inspiration of the Holy Spirit, seemed to think so when he said, "Now may the God of peace himself sanctify you entirely; and may your spirit and soul and body be preserved complete, without blame at the coming of our Lord Jesus Christ. Faithful is he who calls you, and he also will bring it to pass" (1 Thess 5:23–24).

Discipling others is one of the most rewarding ministries one can undertake. First, we have an opportunity to be used by God to change the landscape of eternity. Every person we lead to Christ and every person we disciple changes eternity. As each one grows and serves God, he will contribute to the change because he will now spend his life in service to God, impacting others and earning rewards magnifying the changes to the landscape of eternity. Second, you experience a tremendous joy when you see that person's light of understanding go on, to see his desire for growth feeding his hunger for God. It is a great joy to watch the young believer live a consistent Christian life and one day begin discipling other people. As a discipler, you have obeyed the most important command Christ ever gave his followers—the command to make disciples. Finally, as your disciple becomes a multiplying disciple, multiplying his life into the life of another, you have the opportunity in your circle of influence (as the early church did) to "turn the world upside down." With God's help, may it be so.

REVIEW QUESTIONS

1. What is God's *procedure* for accomplishing his *plan*?
2. List the generations of the discipled, named in the three examples of multiplication the author outlines, as given in the New Testament.
3. What are the three legs or pillars of discipleship and why is each one necessary?

4. List the six characteristics necessary for discipleship as patterned in the ministry of Jesus Christ.
5. The acronym *Father* represents qualities that are necessary when selecting one to disciple. What are they?

7

Reaching the Disenfranchised, Part 1

Helping People Deal with Racial Discrimination, Low Self-esteem, and Depression

IT WAS SUNDAY MORNING and I was just starting my Bible lesson in the Men's Department of the church when Miguel walked in. He sat down in class, drunk and with dried blood all over his face. He had several wounds exposed, one on the side of his head slicing through his ear and another from his nose severing his lip. His gory appearance in class caught everyone's attention and obviously became a major disruption. Miguel refused to go to the hospital, and he would not leave the class. After much persuasion, we finally convinced him to let Mike, one of our leaders, take him to the emergency room.

The ER nurse treated him very roughly, mercilessly digging at his wounds. Seeing Miguel grimace in pain, Mike asked the nurse if she could please be a little gentler. Her look showed intolerance as she continued several more rough scrubbing attempts; humiliated and in pain, Miguel got up and walked out. The next day the police picked him up off the street and took him back to the hospital where he finally got the stitches he needed. Along with these injuries, Miguel has numerous knife scars and bullet wounds received while in a Chicago street gang.

Several years ago Miguel received Christ as his personal Savior and claims to believe in him but does not show the fruit that would assure us that his belief is from the heart. Since I met Miguel about eight years ago, he has been in and out of psychological care facilities and hospital psychiatric wards many times, and has also been in and out of jail. We have taken him to Christian drug and alcohol rehab centers five times, only for him to leave before making it through the induction process. Miguel has disrupted my Sunday class more times than I can remember. I have spent countless hours with Miguel visiting him in the hospital, counseling him, exhorting him, praying for him, and buying him lunch on numerous occasions.

A couple years ago, Miguel kicked out the plate glass windows in the four entry doors at the church where I serve as a pastor. He told me later that he thought our Senior Pastor was being held hostage.

Miguel is one of the millions of men in this country who are disenfranchised. He wants help, he wants to be a father to his son, and he wants to be productive, but he can't escape the bondage he has lived with for the past twenty-nine years. Can we find success in *Rescuing People from Debilitating Strongholds*?

WHO ARE THE DISENFRANCHISED?

Webster's Collegiate Dictionary says to disenfranchise is to deprive of franchise, of a legal right of some privilege or immunity; especially: to deprive of the right to vote.[1]

The colloquial use of the term by society has been broadened to encompass not only some who are literally deprived of some privilege but would include many who feel disenfranchised. Therefore, we are referring here to the disenfranchised as people who may feel they have lost their rights because of the way, rightly or wrongly, they have been treated. Often the treatment has been unfair and discriminatory, brought on because of their lifestyle, practices, race, or condition.

Throughout this chapter, we will see the destructive quality and generational effects of living in a disenfranchised mindset. I agree with Viv Grigg that the cycle often continues from generation to generation: Certain personal sins (drunkenness, drug abuse, sexual immorality, and so on) cause poverty, and poverty is known to causes certain personal sins (stealing, lying, gambling, prostitution, murder, etc.).2 So the disenfranchised often live in that cycle throughout life, with their children repeating the cycle.

Twenty-six years ago my wife and I, along with three young children, moved into the near northwest side of Chicago known as the Humboldt

1. Webster, *Dictionary*, 332.

2. Grigg, *Poor*, 29.

Park community. This is an area of the inner city where many men and women who consider themselves disenfranchised live. We have had the opportunity to know and minister to many of these people.

Under this definition, the disenfranchised may be:

1. Those who have suffered from racial discrimination most of their lives
2. Those with an addiction, especially to alcohol and drugs
3. People who have been released from prison with one or more felony convictions
4. Those men and women practicing homosexuality
5. People who have suffered from physical, sexual, and psychological abuse beginning in childhood
6. Those who are members of street gangs
7. Men or women who were raised without an active relationship with a true father figure

THE FIRST STEP IN HELPING THE DISENFRANCHISED

Prior to delving into the social and psychological factors leading someone to feel disenfranchised, it is necessary to include an overriding and foundational step without which there is little we can do to truly help them. They must put their faith in Jesus Christ as Lord and Savior. Without a new birth experience, there will never be the change of attitude, a desire for growth, and the motivation and hope (coming from God) that one can break the bondage that has towered over them for so many years.

Without new life in Christ, we do not have the Holy Spirit who takes up residence for the purpose of growing and changing us. The Holy Spirit's presence enables the addict to have permanent victory; the one who lost hope can now find new strength and motivation in Christ, and those who have used illegal and immoral means for financial support can find a new way of living, for in Christ all things are possible.

I don't mean to say that the first words out of our mouths must be an attempt to share the gospel. Sometimes it is necessary to start with felt or perceived needs, even though these needs may not be the primary needs in the person's life. Meeting these peripheral needs may often make it possible for one to establish credibility so the person will listen. The real needs are transformational, not just dealing with symptoms. In the final analysis, the spiritual needs are preeminent. It is important to be reminded that helping the disenfranchised will mean little in eternity unless the help we provide becomes a bridge leading to eternal salvation. Holistic ministry is the right method but must always be used as a means to bring the lost to Christ and to help them stand on their own.

SOCIAL AND PSYCHOLOGICAL FACTORS LEADING ONE TO FEEL DISENFRANCHISED

No Relationship with a Father

Other than the absence of a relationship with Jesus Christ as Savior, I know of no factor that more clearly and completely impairs a person's life than the absence of a father. In fact, this characteristic is the common denominator of most of the disenfranchised. Because of the all-encompassing negative influences levied on a person raised without an active father, I have devoted an entire chapter to this topic titled "The Absent Father."

Racial Discrimination

The unrelenting effects of racism have had a venomous effect upon the psyche of many in minority groups. Psychological deprivation and poverty have been key factors in marring the self-image of many minorities, especially those from an African American and Hispanic background. The impact of poor self-esteem lowers one's aspirations and motivation. Often the anger that has come from a poor self-esteem is turned inward on one's self. One begins to believe the bigoted attitudes, feeling worthless and, therefore, having no motivation to better one's self. This explains one reason why alcoholism and drug addiction is so high in African American and Hispanic communities.

How should the Christian respond to racism? Racism is an invention of sinful man. Young children know nothing of racial differences but are taught prejudicial concepts from parents and society. All men were created in the image of God. In Acts 17:26, the Apostle Paul states clearly that, "He made from one man every nation of mankind to live on all the face of the earth." James talks about the attitude we should have toward those who are poor. He says that there should be absolutely no preferential treatment (Jas 2:1–9). In Galatians 3:28, Paul says, "There is neither Jew nor Greek, there is neither slave nor free man, there is neither male nor female; for you are all one in Christ."

A common reaction to racism is anger. People from minority groups often feel that their efforts to achieve are constantly being disallowed by discriminatory behavior from people throughout society. When attempts for success are hindered, anger is the natural response.

The love of Christ controls or compels us to act differently toward others (2 Cor 5:14), helping each one to properly deal with his anger. Anger often consumes the individual so that one is unable to think and act properly. Anger, of course, is an emotion and not a sin. However, if we do not attend to it, anger will quickly become sin, suppressed inward to fester, resulting in hatred and bitterness. We must treat anger as a sin, confessing it to God (1 John 1:9).

In helping those who have suffered from racism, we first of all need to make sure that our lives do not have a hint of prejudice. Be leery of stereotypes, which can often be demeaning. We must be careful that we do not repeat humor that could be interpreted in a prejudicial way. We should be careful that our illustrations do not put any group in a negative light; for example, we must make sure the white guy isn't always the hero or role model in an illustration. To be effective, we must affirm the culture of the person we are trying to reach.

Again, first and foremost, there should not be a trace of prejudice among believers, especially among spiritual leaders. If there is, it will create a major barrier in our quest to reach and disciple those from other ethnic groups. In 1 Timothy 5:21, Paul says, "I solemnly charge you in the presence of God and of Christ Jesus and of his chosen angels, to maintain these principles without bias, doing nothing in a spirit of partiality."

Second, we need to teach how God views people regardless of their race. They were made in God's image and have equal value with all men of every race.

Third, those who have experienced racism need to forgive the unjust and ungodly acts and attitudes expressed against them.

What about racial injustices and how can we have true racial reconciliation in the church? There is no question that many believers from every race are at fault. How do we, as a church, address these issues and be an instrument of love and unity? First, it needs to be foundational in our philosophy, teaching that prejudice against all races and cultures (including prejudice of those with a different social and economic status) should be eradicated. All believers are part of the body of Christ and must be treated and loved as full members. As part of the body of Christ, all believers must be treated equally and fully welcomed to our local assemblies and accepted as members and co-laborers.

I have also learned that when a church becomes multicultural it eliminates most of the prejudicial attitudes. At Armitage Baptist Church, with our thirty-seven different nationalities, we work side by side and learn to truly love and appreciate all races and cultures. There is much said today about the need for classes and instruction on racial reconciliation; however, without de-emphasizing the importance of instruction and dialogue, my experience tells me that the best reconciliation takes place when we worship, serve, fellowship, cry, and laugh with brothers and sisters who differ from us ethnically and/or culturally. When we are exposed to these experiences week after week, our racial and cultural prejudices continually shrink.

The well-known statement that the worst segregated hour in the week is on Sunday morning should grieve us deeply. The church must lead the way in showing love to all men. If the multicultural church is the best environment for true reconciliation, how do we create a multicultural church? Please read the section about the multicultural church in the chapter titled, "Planting an Urban Church." Whether you have scores of different cultures in your community or just two, you can strive to reach them and have those races and cultures as part of your church.

The Problem of Low Self-Esteem

One of the primary reasons that racism so drastically lowers one's self-esteem is because of the denigration many people from minority groups experience early in life. The impact of poor self-esteem lowers one's aspirations and motivation. No wonder the high school drop out rate in African American and Hispanic communities is often as high as 70 percent.

The treatment of people who have low self-esteem is much more difficult than its prevention. The personality of an individual with poor self-esteem has been wounded deeply through emotional experiences, the knowledge of rejection, and the subconscious false belief that he is inferior to others. The result is often self-destructive and may include the excessive use of alcohol or drugs, lack of motivation to find employment, and abusive behavior against others.

People with poor self-esteem often feel worthless, hopeless, depressed, and have periods of rage. The disenfranchised, who usually possess poor self-esteem, have their esteem beaten down constantly because of circumstances of life. Being an alcoholic or homeless, for example, constantly drives down and reinforces the poor self-esteem and strips the person of any dignity they may have left.

What is self-esteem? To understand self-esteem we must first talk about self-image. Self-image is the evaluation one makes of oneself based on outside standards. A negative self-image may be caused by societal standards, especially peer attitudes and treatment. It may also be caused by a subconscious image that one has of oneself because of having been treated in a demoralizing way. This may include emotional, psychological, physical, or sexual abuse. This assortment of outside influences becomes adopted into one's own view of self.

For the true believer in Christ, a healthy self-image is based on God's view of who "I am." It comes from my identity in Christ. First, it is important to know that "I am" important to God. "I am fearfully and wonderfully made" (Ps 139:14), created in his image (Gen 1:26–27), for a purpose much greater than myself. Our purpose for existence is to glorify God (Rom 11:36; 1 Cor 6:20, 10:31) and to serve him, which will literally impact eternity forever. One's image, even though twisted and damaged by sin, affirms an individual's uniqueness among all created beings and, thus, individual worth and importance to God.

Second, God's view of us is shown by the fact that he sent his only son to give his life to purchase our redemption (John 3:16). Though the Father gave his son, Jesus also freely gave his life so we would have eternal life (John 15:13). This great love is a demonstration of our value to God.

Third, I am an adopted child of an infinite and majestic God who chose to love and accept me. Not only does God accept me, but he has made me acceptable (Eph 1:4–6). This has made it possible for him to place me into his family and to give me an eternal inheritance as co-heir with Jesus Christ, my elder brother (Rom 8:17; Eph 3:6). I am part of a chosen race; a royal priesthood; a holy nation (1 Pet 2:9); and I need to view myself as I really am.

Self-esteem is the emotional reaction an individual has to his or her self-image. It is a demonstration of how a person view him or herself. Our goal as believers should not be to create a positive or a negative self-image. A positive self-image based on the world's standards produces pride (Rom 12:3; 1 Cor 10:12). A negative self-image based on the world's standards makes one into a subjective, hopeless, often depressed person with no self-assurance. A self-image based on who "I am" in Christ produces both humility and a strong sense of self-worth. We don't need a good self-image produced by the praise of men coupled with our achievements; we need a biblically accurate self-image based on what God says about who we are—what he says about our real worth.

The Bible is the best resource available in dealing with a believer who is facing a flawed self-image causing them to feel inferior and unable to achieve. The Bible clearly expresses God's view as to the worth of mankind. We also need to challenge the incorrect attitudes prevalent in our society, including false beliefs and stereotypical thinking. Finally, we need to help the affected see that he or she cannot allow the experience of racism, even though it is real and painful, to be an excuse for inaction. An individual can achieve and prosper with self-determination and perseverance, coupled with the help of God.

The Problem of Depression

Seventeen million people in the United States suffer from depression, and it is a common emotion that many disenfranchised experience. It is understandable that when facing any of the psychological and social problems discussed in this chapter, the result is often hopelessness and despair. These overwhelming and disabling emotions sometimes lead to periods of withdrawal and often self-destructive behavior.

Depression, if left unchecked, often follows a decline or downwards spiral, falling through four stages. The first stage is *disappointment* of unmet desires leading to confusion, sadness, and grief. Imagine the lost dreams and dashed hopes that come when one believes he will never have, for example, a happy marriage and family or even a normal life. Many who have begun to believe the societal prejudices inflicted on them feel a great sense of worthlessness. Once the depressed has experienced disappointment, he enters the second stage, which is *discontentment*. He is not happy with his life and sees no way out. There is no hope, and he feels doomed and destined to remain in this condition. Feeling trapped, the depressed person falls into the third stage, the stage of *despair* and *hopelessness*. He now feels doomed to his misery and begins to give up. He simply quits trying, no longer meeting his responsibilities; and whatever effort he attempts may be halfhearted or incomplete. The final stage of the depression spiral is *destructiveness*. The person develops a critical spirit and may become hostile, impulsive, and apathetic. These feelings may lead to suicidal attempts or even homicidal behavior.

Sandy became a believer in Christ years ago, but a series of problems caused her to fall into a deep depression that lasted for six years. She had four children who all spent time in prison, and after the last one went back into prison, coupled with the loss of her job at the age of sixty-six, Sandy fell into a hopeless state in which she accepted the thoughts that no one cared and there was no hope in living. God was with her and used many people from the church, who went to visit and prayed with her, but it was the consistent support and encouragement of her live-in son that God used to bring her out of the pit of despair. Sandy is not unusual but one of hundreds and even thousands in every city that needs help and, at times, faces the temptation to end it all.

Suicide is the thirteenth leading cause of death worldwide,[3] the eleventh in the United States, and the third among U.S. residents aged from fifteen to twenty-four years.[4] In 2003, there were 384,830 nonfatal visits to U.S. hospital for attempted suicides or other self-harm incidents among persons aged 18 and older.[5]

In order to help the depressed climb out of this downward spiral, we need to help him understand that there is hope in God. Psalm 42:11 (NIV) says:

> "Why are you downcast, O my soul?
> Why so disturbed within me?
> Put your hope in God,
> for I will yet praise him,
> my Savior and my God."

How do we help the person who is suffering from depression? Obviously, if the person does not know Jesus Christ as personal Savior, the best and most important step is to lead him to a saving knowledge of

3. Violence and Health, 2002, 185.
4. American Foundation, *Suicide* 2007, 1.
5. OAS Report, *Suicide*, 2008, 1–2.

Jesus Christ. Romans 5:1 tell us that, as believers, we have peace through our Lord Jesus Christ. Below, I have listed twelve helpful tools to enable the person to step out of the bondage of depression.

1. A depressed person should open the shades of his house and let the light in. He should not live in a dark, dingy house. Researchers agree that sunlight can reduce the effects of Seasonal Affective Disorder—more commonly known as seasonal depression. A commonly accepted belief is that the lack of natural chemicals in the body such as serotonin promotes depression. Indirect sunlight entering the eye gate stimulates the body's production and release of this chemical.
2. He should get out of the house, go for a walk, go to church, and force himself to spend time with godly friends. A person suffering from severe depression can stay locked in his house for months and even years at a time. To break the hold that depression has on him, he needs to take steps to change his environment.
3. He should spend time with positive, encouraging people who will lift his spirit.
4. If one is to have consistent victory over depression, it is necessary to read the Bible daily. Colossians 3:16 says, "Let the word of Christ richly dwell within you, with all wisdom, teaching and admonishing one another with psalms and hymns and spiritual songs, singing with thankfulness in your hearts to God."
5. He should listen to positive, uplifting music. The previous verse in Colossians 3:16 also exhorts us to use the valuable tool of music. Research has proven that music has a major effect on our moods.
6. He should pray throughout the day with a thankful spirit. One of the characteristics of a person who is depressed is fatalistic or pessimistic thinking. Philippians 4:6–7 (NIV) says, "Do not be anxious about anything, but in everything, by prayer and petition, with thanksgiving, present your requests to God. And the peace of God, which transcends all understanding, will guard your hearts and your minds in Christ Jesus." Verse six contains an imperative or command, implying that it is disobedient to harbor anxious or worrisome thoughts. These thoughts demonstrate the opposite of faith in a God who provides our needs. We need to practice the

"stop-think approach." Stop the anxious or worrisome thoughts because the previous verse, Philippians 4:5 (NIV), says "[t]he Lord is near" and to present our requests to God. The promised result will be a heart filled with the peace of God.

7. We should encourage the depressed to think about good things. In times of anxiety Paul tells us, "Whatever is true, whatever is honorable, whatever is right, whatever is pure, whatever is lovely, whatever is of good repute, if there is any excellence and if anything worthy of praise, dwell on these things. The things you have learned and received and heard and seen in me, practice these things, and the God of peace will be with you" (Phil 4:8–9). To think about woes or the possible problems that could be faced only reinforces a negative mindset. To aid in thinking on the positive, a regular diet of God's Word along with positive biblically-based Christian literature is extremely helpful.
8. The depressed should meditate on God's Word. Joshua 1:8–9 says, "This book of the law shall not depart from your mouth, but you shall meditate on it day and night, so that you may be careful to do according to all that is written in it; for then you will make your way prosperous, and then you will have success. Have I not commanded you? Be strong and courageous! Do not tremble or be dismayed, for the LORD your God is with you wherever you go."
9. A counselor should confront distorted and irrational thinking, counseling the depressed person to renew his mind (Rom 12:2). Usually, his thinking is faulty. Failed dreams, desires, and aspirations are often idols of the heart. The desire to be successful is not a sin, but sometimes we raise it to such a high level of importance that it becomes more important than God and becomes an idol. The counselor needs to try to discern the root cause so that he can help the person understand and deal with distorted thinking.
10. We should encourage the depressed person to help others. 2 Corinthians 1:3–4 says, "Blessed be the God and Father of our Lord Jesus Christ, the Father of mercies and God of all comfort, who comforts us in all our affliction so that we will be able to comfort those who are in any affliction with the comfort with which we ourselves are comforted by God." There is something revitalizing

about taking our minds off our own woes and putting our efforts into helping another person.

11. He should be reminded that, as a believer, he can find strength and victory in Christ. Philippians 4:13 says, "I can do all things through him who strengthens me."

12. In some cases, one may need specialized help. Depression can come from physiological or biological sources. A doctor may be needed to help make that determination.

Give the depressed hope by giving them your support, encouragement, and counsel, and with prayer; along with God's enablement, victory and wellness can be achieved.

Racial discrimination, low self-esteem, and depression are major strongholds many face causing them to feel disenfranchised. In the next chapter, we will explore the debilitating strongholds of addictive behavior, poverty, and homelessness.

REVIEW QUESTIONS

1. What does the author mean by the disenfranchised, and what groups of people may be included as those who feel disenfranchised?
2. What is the first and most important step in helping people with the severe problems outlined in this chapter?
3. What are the four social and psychological factors leading one to feel disenfranchised?
4. How does racial discrimination impair a person from being a positive and productive member of society?
5. How can a multicultural church be the best instrument to eliminate racial discrimination?
6. What are the four social and psychological factors leading one to feel disenfranchised?

8

Reaching the Disenfranchised, Part 2

Helping People Deal with Addictive Behavior, Poverty, and Homelessness

I DON'T KNOW OF any group of people who have more reason to feel disenfranchised than those who suffer from addictive behavior, poverty, and homelessness. Many of the feelings they carry come from the negative attitudes of society which form the basis for how people respond to them. Among these three groups of people are those who suffer from the results of addictive behavior. They experience one of the greatest strongholds of any condition known to man. Addiction exerts a vice-like grip on its victims, resulting from physiological and/or emotional dependence perpetuating a host of problems that may be health related or that may produce immoral behavior that often results in legal consequences.

There are many things one can be addicted to: cigarettes; food; sex; gambling; stealing; as well as alcohol and drugs, both legal and illegal. Addictions can be rooted in an emotional need, biological dependence, or simply a developed habit. In this section, I will address the most common forms of addiction: alcoholism and drug addiction—though much of this information can be applied to other addictions as well.

It is estimated that 6.6 million children under the age of eighteen years old live in households with at least one alcoholic parent.[1] Approximately one third of all Americans have someone in their family who has been the source of alcohol abuse.[2]

1. National Institute, *Children*, 1990, 1.
2. National Institute, *Alcoholism*, 1990, 1.

Alcohol and drug addiction has ravaged our country. Few people have not been touched by a relative or friend whose family has been decimated by this bondage. While under the influence, the addict is often abusive to himself and others. He or she does not function relationally the way family members desire and need. He is more irritable and self-absorbed and, when intoxicated, is offensive and basically useless. The suffering that these families experience also comes in the form of economic devastation. The money spent on these addictive substances robs the family of the resources that would otherwise be available. This lifestyle often causes the addict to lose employment and, in order to support the addiction, money is sometimes acquired by illegal means, which in turn leads to jail time or, even worse, murder or suicide. And because statistics are so widely known, one need not even elaborate on the lives lost through accidents caused by people driving automobiles while under the influence of alcohol or drugs.

Why do people become addicted to alcohol and drugs? The initial reasons stem from a desire to avoid pain and experience pleasure. Concerning believers and addiction, however, anything to which you are addicted becomes an idol of the heart and must be dealt with as sin. Second, we need to be careful how we treat our body, which is the temple of the Holy Spirit. First Corinthians 6:19–20 says, "Or do you not know that your body is a temple of the Holy Spirit who is in you, whom you have from God, and that you are not your own? For you have been bought with a price: therefore glorify God in your body." Third, we should not be in bondage to anything. Galatians 5:1 says, "It was for freedom that Christ set us free; therefore keep standing firm and do not be subject again to a yoke of slavery." Though this is talking about slavery to the law, the principle still applies that we are not to be in bondage to anything. Ephesians 4:27 (NIV) says, "Do not give the devil a foothold." Don't give the devil control or influence in any part of our lives. We should not be under the bondage of anything except for the bondage of Jesus Christ.

HELPING THE ADDICTED

The first and most important step in helping the addicted is that he must receive Christ as his personal Lord and Savior. Without God's supernatural help, it is extremely difficult to have victory over this type of bondage. I have seen many men and women who have had years (in some cases up to thirty years) of addiction be transformed by Jesus Christ and be completely changed. I disagree with many who say that alcoholism is a disease. When one can lean on the belief that he has a disease, he now has a crutch or an excuse. Instead, we need a relationship with Jesus Christ who will transform our minds and, with our cooperation, give us victory. Addictions are not diseases; they are bondages that come from biological and emotional dependence. Once a person is regenerated, he becomes a new person and can find complete and permanent change. The statement "once an alcoholic always an alcoholic" is absolutely false. In 1 Corinthians 6:9–11, the Apostle Paul talks about people with various types of bondages and lifestyles who were changed. Paul tells us, "Or do you not know that the unrighteous will not inherit the kingdom of God? Do not be deceived; neither fornicators, nor idolaters, nor adulterers, nor effeminate, nor homosexuals, nor thieves, nor the covetous, nor drunkards, nor revilers, nor swindlers, will inherit the kingdom of God. Such were some of you; but you were washed, but you were sanctified, but you were justified in the name of the Lord Jesus Christ and in the Spirit of our God." He says, "Such were some of you." After salvation they ceased being an alcoholic and they were truly changed: "The old things passed away; behold, new things have come" (2 Cor 5:17).

The second step that is necessary for an addict to take is to admit that he has an addiction. Often those who have an addiction to a substance, such as alcohol, live in denial. They must come to a place in their lives where they admit they need help. Until the believer admits to the addiction and realizes it is his responsibility and his sin, he will never be able to have real victory.

Third, he must be determined to break the addiction. God will help the believer, but he will not force him. He must be determined, with God's enablement, to permanently abstain from any alcohol or drug consumption.

Fourth, he must understand the long-range consequences of his behavior. Addiction is based on immediate gratification, focusing on the craving and enjoyment. Often the addict does not understand or anticipate the long-range consequences he will face. These consequences destroy the family, relationships, health, future productivity, and the person's spiritual relationship with the Lord. The believer who is an addict will also face the chastening hand of the Lord, which comes from God's loving correction.

Fifth, we must develop a strategy to help the addict have complete recovery. For many people, chemical dependence requires a rehabilitation program that may include residential treatment. The most effective Christian programs include an in-depth residential program of spiritual development. Assuming one is a believer, important elements of successful, non-residential rehabilitation from addiction include:

Confession and repentance. As mentioned above, a common characteristic of addiction is denial. Since addiction and any form of bondage is a sin, confession and repentance are foundational. This includes the confession (admission) to God of the specific sin (1 John 1:9) and a decision to turn away from or renounce the sin and sinful lifestyle, and not call it just "a problem" or "a disease" (Prov 28:13).

Prayer for deliverance. Simple willpower is not enough to beat chemical dependence or any controlling addiction. It requires the supernatural power of God who can and will help the believer who has a submissive spirit. Therefore, the believer with an addiction should pray to God for strength, determination, deliverance, and for God to keep him from this temptation. It is truly a blessing to watch our God help those who seriously desire deliverance from bondage.

Staying away from the old environment. The person who is struggling for deliverance from any form of addiction must stop associating with the old friends that aided and encouraged the addiction. This is necessary, especially in the early stages, when the addict is weak and vulnerable. When the former addict goes back to the old neighborhood, he will invariably run into one or more of his old buddies who will offer him a drink or encourage him to hang out with his old friends, "just once, for old time's sake." 1 Corinthians 15:33 says, "Do not be deceived: 'Bad company corrupts good morals.'" One of the greatest devices Satan will use against someone struggling to have victory from drugs or alcohol is his old environment. Therefore, it is crucial that he severs these destructive relationships and resolves to avoid the old hangout spots.

Creating a new environment. When the negative friends and activities are removed, it is necessary to replace them with the kind of relationships and activities that will lift and encourage. Regular attendance in a Bible-believing church is extremely important. I don't mean once a week, but as often as possible. We should make sure that he is in programs and Bible studies where he will develop Christian friends. Small group Bible studies are very helpful for one who is seeking to break bondages because they enable him to build friendships and accountability structures. Opportunities to serve will also provide a way to fill one's time with God-honoring activities that will give him a sense of worth and productivity.

Finding a mentor or discipler. We cannot overemphasize the importance of spiritual growth for the one who seeks victory from any addictive behavior. Discipleship is most effective if it includes a one-on-one relationship with a discipler. The discipler should meet with the addict on a regular basis (if possible more often at first) and be available by phone for encouragement and counsel. A regular series of Bible studies should be followed, including topics that will help the person lay a foundation for spiritual growth. (See the two chapters on discipleship called "Calibrating Our Compass" and "Turn the World Upside Down" for more details.) The discipler will help him to receive and walk in the deliverance that is his in Christ. This deliverance must include regular accountability. It is also necessary that the discipler help the person to understand God's forgiveness. After receiving forgiveness, he is no longer guilty and no longer needs to carry the lifelong stigma of being an addict. According to 1 Corinthians 6:9–11, as stated earlier, these drunkards, along with the rest, no longer carried the stigmatic classification. They were new people in Christ Jesus.

Filling life with productive activity. Productive activity will help the person remain clean from destructive habits. The folk proverb that states "idle hands are the Devil's workshop" contains a lot of truth for the person trying to break the bonds of addiction. We should try to involve him in as many activities as possible. Immerse him in Christ-honoring programs and give him opportunities to serve. Help him realize that there is hope. As he discovers that God can use him, he will gain a sense of motivation to continue this journey.

Sam came to our Sunday Bible study about six years ago. He had his first drink at age five when his brother gave him a glass, telling him it was Kool-Aid. By the age of seven he was addicted, an addiction which lasted thirty-one years. One of our men invited him out to lunch and shared the gospel with him. Sam received Christ that day, but as with many who have an addiction, did not experience immediate deliverance. Though he tried to quit, he continued to struggle. Several men from his class began to encourage him. We were able to enroll and graduate him from a new believers' class. After about nine months of encouragement and instruction, Sam finally repented from the addiction and decided that, with God's help, he would never drink again. We followed the steps listed above, and Sam has now been free from alcohol for over five years. God has truly changed his life from a drunk on the street to a growing man of God. You will find Sam, most days, spending his spare time passing out tracts and witnessing on the streets of Chicago or serving with our church's mercy ministry. Becoming a baptized member of our church, his love for God serves as a contagious example to many other men in our church and community.

When Sam was in his early stages of recovery, we encouraged him to fill his time with productive activity and service. He followed our advice and began coming to:

- Worship on Sunday morning
- Bible Study in the Men's Class after Worship
- Sunday evening new believers class
- Sunday night praise service
- Monday evening Bible study for men that our church hosts
- Tuesday evening tutoring program for children, as an assistant
- Wednesday morning meeting with me for accountability and encouragement
- Early Wednesday evening new believers' class—repeating this class several times for reinforcement and additional encouragement
- Wednesday night prayer meeting
- Thursday morning food pantry ministry attendant
- Saturday afternoon witnessing and passing out tracts with several men from our church

As you can see, Sam kept himself busy.

Though we exhorted and encouraged him to do all these things, he also did them willingly. Granted, everyone seeking freedom from bondages may not have the time to do all the things that Sam did, but the point remains: It is critically important to kept oneself busy when breaking a major addiction.

Don't be discouraged if or when there is a relapse. First Peter 5:8 tells us that Satan is a roaring lion seeking someone to devour. Our cunning adversary knows exactly where our weak areas are. He will use the weakness of the recovering addict every chance he gets. Many times I have seen men who are trying to have victory over their addiction fall back into drugs or alcohol use, but with perseverance and help are able to make it.

William came to me as a new believer who was also breaking a heavy alcohol and drug addiction. He began coming to our new believers' class and quickly displayed a sincere hunger for God. Like many new believers, he couldn't get enough—hanging on every word, writing down much of what I said in his notebook. About two months after his salvation, William had a relapse. Satan simply unloaded both barrels to try to end the change and progress in his life. Our Good Shepherd went after his lost sheep, convicted him, and brought him to full repentance. We began meeting on a regular basis for discipleship. It has now been over seven years and William has not returned to his bondage. William married a wonderful member of our church, has been blessed with three children, and has graduated from a Christian graduate school. Currently, William is a full time staff member at my church.

Many times our Good Shepherd will expect us to go after the lost sheep. When we are working with someone who has a recent history of substance abuse, we need to keep a watchful eye on any hint of sliding. If he begins missing appointments or church services, we need to immediately find out why. Just when you think he has kicked the habit once and for all, Satan attacks again, often laying in wait for a weak moment.

Be alert to times when the person trips into a sinkhole. Sinkholes are mood-altering circumstances or events that create a desire to escape. Sometimes it only takes one of these sinkholes; for other people it is a combination. The wise counselor helps him cope with the stresses that often lead to destructive behavior.

Watch out for *the sinkhole of discouragement*. This may be discouragement over the inability to get or keep a job or the pain experienced over a failed relationship with a person of the opposite sex. It could include financial difficulties, which often comes from financial mismanagement.

The sinkhole of anxiety brings worry and fear of the unknown. We need to quickly help this person practice the "stop-think approach" mentioned under the section on depression in chapter 7, which is based on Philippians 4:6–7. We are commanded not to worry or be anxious about anything. Instead, we are instructed to pray to God for our concerns. It is wonderful to have our anxieties removed when we trust God for our help.

The sinkhole of sin has its own feeling of failure. When we have broken fellowship, we must immediately restore our relationship with the Lord through confession of sin (1 John 1:9). Without restoration to the Lord, our sin will invariably lead to additional sins, beginning a downward spiral.

We need to also watch out for *the sinkhole of failure and disappointment.* This may come from the loss of a job, separation or divorce from a spouse, or problems with children. This sinkhole includes great disappointment that the events in our life and our performance have not measured up to our dreams and expectations. As the person begins to engage in self-absorbed, self-pitying thinking coupled with negative events in one's life, the person finds himself driven into the downward spiral of depression that may be very difficult to overcome. We need to counsel him against negative thinking and encourage him to put his confidence in Jesus Christ who never disappoints.

Once discovered, the counselor needs to help him face and deal with each of these sinkholes, hopefully preventing a slide back to the former addictive behavior.

POVERTY

People who are poor characteristically experience all types of social and family problems. These problems sometimes cause more poverty and create new problems in the home and in family life. The African American community is one minority group with a high percentage of members struggling with poverty. One of the reasons for this poverty is because the average African American income is 56 percent of that of the average income of Whites,[6] forcing many families to have other family members—like siblings, adult children, grandparents, and other relatives—live with them in order to pool resources just to make ends meet. This extended family structure causes all types of problems within the home.

Why is there so much unemployment in the inner city? As Sociologist David Claerbaut stated, the jobs in the want ad section of the paper are not jobs for the poor:

> First, many of these jobs require a substantial amount of education. Even the jobs that require less formal education still require well-developed literary skills. These requirements eliminate most of the poor. Second, many of the factory jobs listed are not located close to the poverty area. Many industries have moved to the suburbs. Third, of these jobs that remain, many pay the minimum wage. At the minimum wage times forty hours, the vast majority of low-income families earn below the federal poverty level. In addition, job related expenses such as travel, perhaps babysitting, clothes, and other mundane items, make it even less economical to accept such employment.[3]

Many poor, inner city residents do not have bank accounts for checking or savings. Therefore, most transactions are done in cash. In order to pay bills and conduct other business, one is forced to deal with a currency exchange, which charges high service fees. In Chicago, such services include cashing checks, issuing money orders, paying utility bills, purchasing a required automobile city sticker, license plate, bus and subway passes, food assistance cards or stamps, as well as other services.

As Michael Allen said, "Perhaps the number one root cause of poverty that I have uncovered is open and willful rebellion against every God-ordained institution of society (family, government, church, and work). These institutions are like a big umbrella of life that serves as a shelter and support during all stages of life if we learn to respectively use it as designed."[4]

An underlying reason for much poverty is the lack of a father in the home. According to the U.S. Census Bureau, Annual Social and Economic Supplement, in 2007 fatherless children were more than five times as likely as children living in households headed by married parents to be living in poverty. Combining children of all races, the poverty rate for children in single mother households was 42.9 percent compared with 8.5 percent for children in married households.[5]

3. Claerbaut, *Urban*, 74.
4. Allen, *Heart for City*, 221–222.
5. Census Bureau, 2008.

As you can see, the problems associated with poverty produce insurmountable obstacles that can only be scaled with the help and grace of God.

HOMELESSNESS

"There are an estimated four to five million homeless people in the United States, and most of them live on the streets of our large cities."[6] According to the 1995 U.S. Conference of Mayors Report, 46 percent of homeless people in America are men. Homeless people are the poorest of the poor, destitute, and unwanted. They can be seen begging outside supermarkets, sleeping in doorways and on park benches. They may be found picking through dumpsters and holding up signs at intersections asking for help. There are more than one hundred million street children in today's world-class cities around the world—25 percent of whom both work and sleep in the streets.[7]

It is easy to understand why there are so many homeless people in third world cities, but why are there so many homeless people in the United States? Homelessness is caused by many factors. One factor is mental illness. According to the U.S. government, estimates of two hundred thousand homeless people are mentally ill, which equals one third of the homeless population.[8]

A second reason an affluent country such as the United States has so many homeless people is the lack of affordable housing for the poor. In the past forty years, many low-cost housing apartments have been demolished with only a small percentage being replaced. The number of poor people has increased while the affordable housing has decreased. Between 1973 and 1993, 2.2 million low-rent units disappeared from the market in the United States. These units were condemned, burned, abandoned, or converted into condominiums and expensive apartments. The apartments that remain standing became unaffordable because of the increase in rent. During the same period, the number of low-income renters increased by 4.7 million.[9]

6. Greenway and Monsma, *Cities,* 180.

7. Myers, *Missions*, 42.

8. Adair, *Lighthouse*, 105.

9. Lazare, Housing Gap, 1995.

A third factor leading to homelessness is poor self-esteem—a belief that someone is incapable of holding down a job or succeeding in the normal world. This discourages the homeless from looking for employment.

A fourth factor that affects homelessness is the widespread use of chemical substances made possible by the availability of cheap alcohol and crack cocaine. It is clear that something must be done, and I believe the only effective solution is found in Jesus Christ.

REACHING AND MINISTERING TO THE DISENFRANCHISED

As we have indicated previously, the number of people classified as disenfranchised is astronomical, especially in large cities. These people carry many problems and struggle with numerous strongholds. How do we begin to impact these people for whom Christ died? There are several basic principles that are foundational; without them, long-term effectiveness will be minimal.

The Importance of the Local Church in Ministering to the Disenfranchised

In my years of serving Christ I have observed many personal and organizational Christian ministries that have diligently worked to reach and minister to the disenfranchised. I applaud their work and have learned much from their efforts. But I am absolutely persuaded that the most effective organization to have long-term impact is the local church. Granted, many local churches have failed to meet this need, but it is still God's ordained institution to impact all people regardless of their problems and needs. Many have tried to reach people, apart from the church without making an intentional effort to integrate them into a thriving body.

There are several reasons why the church is indispensable in any effective ministry to the disenfranchised. The first and most important reason is the step of helping the disenfranchised move toward salvation and then growth to maturity. As they begin growing, the Holy Spirit will give grace to meet their trials, convict and restore them as they sin, guide in the decision making process, transform their lives into people who have a commitment to Jesus Christ as Lord, and help them actively serve him. Without that foundation and spiritual development, the success rate would be dismal. The church is called and ordained by God for that very purpose. One may think he can reach a person for Christ and disciple him apart from the local church. I will admit that he may reach a person for Christ, but complete discipleship cannot take place apart from the church. For the sake of obedience alone (Heb 10:24–25), the believer needs to become a member and actively serve the Lord in the local church.

A second reason why the church is indispensable in effective ministering to the disenfranchised is that it can meet one of their desperate needs: replacing their negative environment with an environment that includes positive God-honoring relationships that will encourage and support them in the process of transformation.

Third, God has designed the church with an accountability system through its members. The church also has the organizational structure to exercise church discipline. This is very needful to help each of us walk that straight and narrow path. As a pastor I have seen many people who have moved out of state, going to an area where they were unable to find a church they felt comfortable with. Within a year of non-attendance they found themselves in a backslidden state and often with one of the marriage partners in the middle of an affair. Often, reconciliation never takes place and the couple's life is altered forever. It is of great value to place oneself under the authority and watchful care of a pastor within a local church that provides accountability between its members and corporate accountability through church discipline.

Fourth, the church is designed by God to be a school for the saints. It is a teaching and training center that will equip, motivate, and empower its members to serve Christ (Eph 4:11–15). To aid this process, the Holy Spirit distributes spiritual gifts to believers at salvation for the purpose of edifying the body of Christ (1 Cor 12:11, 14:12; Eph 4:10).

Fifth, the church provides a place where we can participate in regular worship and study of his Word. God is so committed to the church as the only institution to accomplish his purpose for this age that he made Jesus to be the head of it (Col 1:18). It is referred to as his body (Eph 4:12; Rom 7:4; 1 Cor 10:16) and his church (Matt 16:18). As such, we should put ourselves in complete support and commitment to a church that is faithful to God's Word so as to serve him in his body. For the same reason we must make every effort to help the disenfranchised become a part of the local church as well.

Live Where They Live—Incarnational Ministry

When working with people of other cultures, it is important to understand that every individual has a worldview unique to his culture. Worldview is composed of attitudes, values, and opinions. They affect how we think, make decisions, and define events. If you don't understand the culture, you will face many roadblocks as you try to communicate and minister. In a large city there are thousands of cultures, with ethnicity being only one determining factor. Other factors that impact culture include economic level, language, and morality.

In the chapter titled "Principles of Urban Ministry," I developed this point along with a number of other important values that are vital to an effective urban ministry. Suffice it to say that you will never have the respect and long-term impact, especially in this country, unless you live where they live or in a similar environment not far away.

Develop a Personal Ministry

How do you reach the disenfranchised? You reach them one at a time, and that means you must get personally involved in their lives. I would like to share with you ten suggestions that, if practiced, will enable you to have great success in reaching urban people, especially the disenfranchised.

First, *you must love and accept them.* Love is the universal language. By love, I am not talking about a feeling. I am talking about the highest form of love referred to in the Greek language by the word *agapao*, which we refer to as agape love. This is "an unconditional commitment to an imperfect person." One of my respected seminary professors, Dr. Victor Matthews, of Grand Rapids Baptist Theological Seminary, defined agape love as " decision to recognize another person as a person, to give that person rightful place in my life, and to do the right thing by him." I don't always feel love; the feeling is an occasional byproduct. My responsibility is to make a decision and to act on that decision. That's how I can love my enemies (Matt 5:44). I don't have to like them, but I can make a decision to love them, treating each one as a person. God created the alcoholic, drug addict, and homeless person in his image. Not only did he create them in his image, but he also sent his Son to die for them. They are not animals; we must treat them with dignity and respect for who they really are. To "give them rightful place in our life and to do the right thing by them" means that if I claim Jesus as my Lord, then the people he created in his image and died for have a rightful place in my life. I must act on what God wants me to do in relationship to them. That does not mean that we let people take advantage of us, and it does not mean we do and give them everything they ask for. Agape love is sometimes demonstrated with a positive action and other times it is expressed with a negative response. I discipline my children because I love them. This is a negative expression but, nonetheless, is the right thing for me to do.

In our fast-paced, busy schedule we are always looking for short-cuts and quick solutions. An expression of agape love is not necessarily a quick action and is often inconvenient. When Jesus said that we should love our neighbor as our self (Matt 22:39), he was telling us that it is a high priority, probably higher than most of the urgent tasks pressing in on us. If we expect to reach the disenfranchised, we need to consistently practice agape love. That is very difficult; but what God has commanded, he will enable.

Second, *be available to them, making time in your schedule.* Divine appointments are seldom convenient. I have a standing agreement with the receptionist that she can always call me when someone comes to our church needing counsel or help. The person requesting help may attend our services or come from outside the church; some are the disenfranchised. I treat these opportunities as divine appointments. God has used these occasions to lead people to himself for salvation, to restore others in their relationship with him, and for some, my divine appointment has become a port of entry to someone seeking a church. One such divine appointment resulted in an opportunity for me to lead a man to Christ and disciple him one-on-one for a period that lasted one-and-a-half years. He is now an active, serving member of our church. We must realize the importance of making ourselves available.

Third, *be patient with the disenfranchised.* It took many years for them to get to their current state, so we must not expect instant results. I have found that I need to pray for them, love them, and, often, God gives glimpses of hope. Sometimes it seems like we are on a sand dune, with two steps forward and sliding one step back. But if we faithfully persevere, God will provide amazing breakthroughs. The key word is perseverance. You may ask whether spending all this time is good stewardship. Jesus seemed to think so. In Matthew 25:31–46, he said if we give food to the hungry, a drink to the thirsty, housing for the homeless, care for the sick, and we visit those in prison, it is as though we did these things to Jesus himself. He had great compassion for the disenfranchised, and we are to walk in his footsteps.

Fourth, *meet their perceived needs when possible.* This will often become a bridge to reach them. The disenfranchised are not always open to our spiritual ministry and may not be open to the gospel. Repeated attempts sometimes fall on deaf ears, and an insensitive approach may even cause them to be bitter toward you. Beginning with their perceived needs often opens the door for a spiritual ministry.

Remember the example of Jesus with the disenfranchised woman at the well (John 4:7–26). When he approached her, he asked her for a drink. She had suffered much rejection; first, because she was a Samaritan; second, because she was a woman; and then, of course, because of her immoral lifestyle. Asking the woman for a drink from her cup demonstrated acceptance. He was demonstrating agape love to her, treating her as a person. The need for acceptance and love represents one of her deepest perceived needs.

Fifth, *provide role models for the disenfranchised.* Because of the lack of God-honoring, adult role models, there is a desperate need for the church to provide these examples. There is a great need for good disciplers and mentors who become father figures. There is a need for good families to model the Christian home, Christian husband and wife relationships, model how to be a godly father or mother, and for training parents on how to rear and discipline their children. There is a great need for Christian male leadership that is spiritually consistent, modeling men of integrity.

Sixth, *help the disenfranchised become self-sufficient.* You have heard the saying: "Give a man a fish, and you feed him for a day; teach him how to fish, and you feed him for a lifetime." If our ministry ends with a bowl of soup, we have done an injustice to the person in need. If we can encourage and help him get a job, we not only have provided a way for his ongoing needs to be met, but we have provided a means of self-respect. The liberal welfare mentality he has grown to be a part of has caused severe damage to the worldview of many disenfranchised. What is needed is not always charity. It is often better to provide an opportunity to work so that the disenfranchised can provide for themselves. Even when there is a legitimate financial need, an opportunity can be created in which the person does a specific amount of work in order to earn the money. This step may be necessary to help the person become self-sufficient.

Seventh, *there is a time for tough love.* Don't help them sin by being an enabler. Giving a quarter to a panhandler may be enabling the person to continue in their addiction. When an alcoholic asks for money, I routinely tell him no, that it would not help him. I may, however, decide to buy him lunch if I believe that providing food is the right thing for me to do as an expression of agape love.

Eighth, *we must have credibility and integrity.* If I have no credibility or integrity no one will listen to me. Webster's Collegiate Dictionary says that to have credibility means, "to be sufficiently good to bring esteem or praise."[10]My life must measure up to my message. Integrity has to do with a firm adherence to moral values. If I say I will meet someone at a certain time, I need to be there. If I agree to do something, I need to keep my word and come through with my promise. If I have an appointment with someone, I cannot take the day off or make other plans unless I contact the party first and make other arrangements. We need to be men and women of integrity if we expect to instill the respect and confidence that is necessary to have an eternal impact on those to whom we minister.

Ninth, *lead them to Christ.* To some, this will be obvious. One of the tendencies of urban ministry is to provide all kinds of social or holistic services. These services are good and often necessary if we are to reach them, but our ministry must not end with the social provision. All the feeding, job training, and provision of housing is useless if the person spends a Christless eternity in hell. The important thing to be reminded of is that unless we make a concerted and planned effort to pray and share the gospel with them, this vital step will be crowded out with all other urgent needs and pressures. If we are serious about a desire to lead them to Christ, we must be there during times of tragedy and extreme stress such as the death of a loved one, hospitalization due to a serious illness or accident, or some other form of tragedy. Often holistic ministries leave this ingredient out. If we are there at the time of crisis, God will soften their heart to be receptive to the gospel.

Tenth, *help them grow spiritually.* A baby needs to be bottle-fed and then spoon-fed. Eventually, he begins to feed himself but still needs

10. Webster, *Dictionary*, 272.

some guidance until he has grown to maturity. That requires a lot of time and effort on the part of the parent. Spiritual parenting also takes time and an extreme amount of effort. Perhaps that is why few ministries truly disciple the people they reach. We simply invite them to our services. The new convert needs to be taught the basic, foundational truths first and then more advanced teaching. Being in a relationship with a discipler is extremely valuable and indispensable in the growth process. He will provide a model to follow, encouragement, counseling, instruction, and accountability. One who is discipled in this way will grow in a year as much as it would have taken ten years to grow by just attending services. Discipleship ministry does not take the place of the church; it is the ministry of the church, the Great Commission.

Each of these personal ministry suggestions is critical if we are going to have true success in reaching urban people, especially the disenfranchised.

Commit to a Ministry for a Long Period of Time—Longevity

It's a struggle for a mountaineer to climb to a high summit. He must deny himself, suffer pain, fight the desire to turn back, and persevere until the prize has been achieved. Similar struggles and obstacles await the disenfranchised if he is to climb the barriers before him. One of the biggest needs of the mountain climber is support. He cannot do it alone without a partner. For the disenfranchised, to climb out of his valley of discouragement, defeat, and pain takes perseverance and determination. He must have the support of a partner and, without the help of a gracious God, there is little hope for success.

The disenfranchised person has usually experienced an unstable life. He may not know his father; his mother has a temporary boyfriend; and his mother and he and his siblings, have moved from one apartment to the next. The entire experience of the disenfranchised is unstable; therefore, he desperately needs consistency and stability. The church needs to provide stability, and the pastor and church workers need to be a part of this stable picture. This cannot be accomplished with the short tenure so common with pastors and church staff in the United States.

Many times the person who God has touched may drift away. He may be a non-believer or he may have received Christ, but because of Satan's hold on him, he may backslide. As God continues to draw him to salvation or, as a believer under God's corrective and chastening hand, he will eventually come back looking for the person whom God used to impact his life. What if the person who has ministered to him completes his brief stint and moves on? Who will continue the process? Longevity is critically important in any ministry, but it is all the more needed in an urban setting. People in ministry need to weather the storms, persevering in the same location. If we serve for an extended period of time in the same ministry, the blessings and the fruit that come from service will be far greater than for the worker or pastor who has many short-term ministries. It takes time to reach the disenfranchised, and you will begin to see fruit only after an extended period, usually years.

Your Ministry Must Be Supernatural

We have the same God that created the universe and the same God who parted the Red Sea for Moses and the Children of Israel. This same God tells us that with the faith of a mustard seed we can move mountains. But some seem to think we are in a different age, an age in which God does not demonstrate supernatural power. God has not changed. He does want to work in and through us in a supernatural way today, and we need his supernatural power in reaching men and women with so many destructive habits and problems.

If anything lasting is going to take place in a ministry to the disenfranchised, it will be because of him, not us. That means God's servants need to bathe what they do in prayer. Only God can change a life, and that is why his servants are in this business in the first place. Your ministry can be supernatural as you keep your life pure and depend on him for the results. For a review of this, read Principle Seven: Urban Ministry Must Be Supernatural, in chapter 4, "Principles of Urban Ministry."

REVIEW QUESTIONS

1. What is the first and most important step to take that will enable a person to live free from an addiction?
2. Assuming one is a believer, what are seven important elements of successful, non- residential, drug or alcohol rehabilitation?
3. What are the three reasons stated for so much unemployment in the inner city?
4. What are the four causes for homelessness stated in the chapter?
5. Why is the church so important in helping the disenfranchised?

9

The Absent Father

The Greatest Problem in Our Society

OTHER THAN THE ABSENCE of a relationship with Jesus Christ as Savior, I know of no factor that more clearly and completely impairs so many people's lives than the absence of a father in the home.

In his own words, Carlos shares the vacuum left when raised in a home without a father:

> I come from a large family. There are seven of us. I have three brothers and three sisters to be exact, and I am smack dab in the middle of them all. My mother raised us by herself. We grew up on welfare. I don't recall ever thinking of ourselves as poor or lacking anything. This was just how things were. My father left our family when I was four years old. I can remember only two or three memories of him. Most of my friends and neighbors were in the same situation. My life's circumstances were not at all unique. Still, in a remarkable way, the absence of my father weighed heavily on me throughout my childhood and even into adulthood. Somehow it felt as if I was the only one in my family and community who was suffering over a father's abandonment. It was certainly difficult walking around feeling disconnected from everyone.
>
> I wish I could say that after I became a Christian, the void my Dad left was somehow immediately filled, but it wasn't. Yes, I was saved, rescued, and given a new life. However, the hard work of healing had just begun. After getting married, I used to wonder when the moment would come when I would walk away and leave my family. It haunted me; I felt that abandoning them was my lot in life. What was so amazing is that even though I didn't know my father, I felt like I was becoming more and more like

> him. God slowly began to show me that what I viewed as normal was anything but. He showed me that men can be tough but kind. That men can care and not be cold and indifferent. That men can be constructive, not destructive. And the truth that I believe is the most important for me, now that I am a father, is that fathers can stay.
>
> True fathers don't leave, they gut it out. Life gets hard, at times it may feel unbearable, but we stay. We use God's strength not ours. I used to pray "God give me strength," but now I pray "God keep me weak, but give me your strength." My strength fades, I get exhausted, but God never does. I long ago reconciled myself to the fact that my Dad was not coming back for me, he's gone. I am thirty-nine years old now with a wonderful, patient, tough wife, and together we have seven children. Have I gained ground? Yes, but slowly. Gaining ground is a continuing process. Just when I think I have made it, God reveals more things that I need to work on. Aren't we all a continued work in progress? But so much is at stake. Being a father is a high calling. In fact, I believe it is one of the highest callings. I am confident that God is going to break this legacy of abandonment with me. I will be a father to them by more than just being there. I will give them spiritual guidance, love, security, discipline, laughter, and joy. I will be there to help them through their pain, and I will be there at those moments of victory. Because . . . I'm staying.

Carlos made it, but the vast majority of young men and women don't, and those who do carry with them a suitcase full of deep wounds and many mistakes, bring a myriad of consequences and an assortment of baggage.

Our culture is in deep trouble. Anyone can look around and see the effects of this problem on our society. The astounding debilitating impact the absentee father leaves is eye opening. In fact, this characteristic is the common denominator in most of the disenfranchised talked about in the last chapter. As Viv Grigg said, "Fatherless children are at a dramatically greater risk of drug and alcohol abuse, mental illness, suicide, poor educational performance, teen pregnancy, and criminality."[1]

The following statistics overwhelmingly support the above claim:

- 63 percent of youth suicides are from fatherless homes
- 90 percent of all homeless and runaway children are from fatherless homes

1. Grigg, *Poor*, 29.

- 85 percent of all children that exhibit behavioral disorders come from fatherless homes
- 71 percent of all high school dropouts come from fatherless homes
- 85 percent of rapists motivated with displaced anger come from fatherless homes
- 85 percent of all youths sitting in prisons grew up in fatherless homes
- 75 percent of all adolescent patients in chemical abuse centers come from fatherless homes[2]

The blame for crime has often been misplaced. As stated by Douglas A. Smith and G. Roger Jarjoura in the article titled *Social Structure and Criminal Victimization*, "Criminologists have long used race and poverty as key variables for explaining crime rates. However, researchers at the University of Maryland find that when differences in family structures are taken into account, crime rates run much the same in rich and poor neighborhoods and among African American, White, and Hispanic populations."[3] Thus, the problems come, not so much from poverty and race, as they do from the lack of a father in the home.

The lack of a father in the home is a national epidemic. Four out of every ten children in the United States will go to sleep in homes where their fathers do not live. Before they reach the age of eighteen, more than half of America's children are likely to spend at least a significant portion of their childhood living apart from their fathers.[4]

The impact of fatherless homes affects our country but all the more degrade our cities. According to the research done by A. Anne Hill and June O'Neill published in an article titled *Underclass Behaviors in the United States*, the likelihood that a young male will engage in criminal activity doubles if he is raised without a father and triples if he lives in a neighborhood with a high concentration of single-parent families.[5]

The city of Chicago has an average of 13 percent of all babies being born to teenagers. The neighborhood in Chicago where I live, Humboldt Park, has an annual birth rate of 29 percent of babies born to teenagers.

2. Department of Justice, *Report*, 11.
3. Smith and Jarjoura, *Victimization*, 220.
4. Morehouse, *Father*, 6.
5. Hill and O'Neill, *Underclass,* 1993.

The adjoining neighborhoods of West Town and Logan Square have 20 percent and 19 percent respectively.[6] The large number of single mothers raising families usually insures the prevalence of poverty, creating problems of inadequate housing, inadequate health care, poor childcare, and, often, dependence on welfare.

Today in America two out of every five children grow up fatherless.

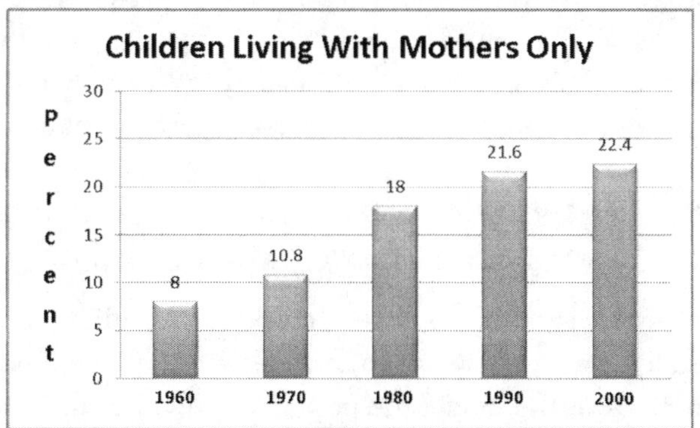

Census document: CH-1. Living Arrangements of Children Under 18: 1960 to Present. Internet Release Date: January 7, 1999. http://www.census.gov/population/socdemo/ms-la/tabch-1.txt.

The problem of absentee fathers is even greater in the city. The 1997 Gallup Youth Survey found the following among U.S. teens: 33 percent live away from their fathers, but 43 percent of urban teens live away from their fathers.[7]

The lack of a father in the home negatively impacts the childrens' worldviews. First, it often leaves children with a distorted view of the intact family structure that God intended, causing the children to grow up not knowing what a good marriage looks like, and how to be a father. Second, in many cases it lends itself to poor parental discipline. Third, one's experience with a father image, which is usually lacking or negative at best, colors the subconscious view of God who is often referred to as our Heavenly Father. Finally, because there are few examples of good male role models and few examples of good marriages, it becomes difficult to develop productive adults and strong marriages as well as good male leadership.

6. Mead, *Kids*, 454.

7. National Center for Fathering, Gallop, 1997.

A young lady is automatically identified as a woman when she is able to have children and especially when she bears her first child, but when does a boy become a man?

In many cultures in our world there is a specific time, a clear-cut occasion, when a boy becomes a man. What is the age or event in America, and what celebration surrounds this important rite of passage? When he gets a driver's license? When he joins the army? Does he become a man when he takes a woman to bed? Does he become a man when he can provide financially for himself? Our society is very ambiguous about these issues. Boys are left to grapple with a blurred concept of identity.

THREE SOURCES OF INFLUENCE THAT AFFECT OUR SOCIETY'S VIEW OF MASCULINITY

The first source that affects our society's view of masculinity is *the family.* Historically, the father was a critical piece in the manhood puzzle. He was the head of the home, the protector, provider, and leader. He provided a clear view of masculinity and provided affirmation to the young man growing up. His presence also provided clarity to his female children. A mature Christian father helped each of his children plainly see what a man was like and how one was to treat his wife. They could clearly see what marriage was supposed to be like.

Unfortunately, as I have demonstrated, this primary and vital training source is absent from a large number of homes. To add to this problem, in many homes where there is a father present he is detached and distant. Some struggle with addictions, others are workaholics and spend little time with their children. Our culture is in deep trouble, and the heart of the problem is the loss of vision and example of masculinity.

The second source is *the community.* The culture of many countries has a clear understanding when a boy becomes a man and treats him as a man with a "rite of passage." One good illustration is in the Jewish culture with the concept of bar mitzvah, a celebration that occurs at the age of thirteen, the age a Jewish boy becomes a man. Jewish children are not allowed to read from the Torah. During this ceremony in the Synagogue, the thirteen year old young man is allowed to read as an adult man marking his first time doing so as an adult.

Luke 2:42–52 records Jesus going to Jerusalem with his parents. With the concept of bar mitzvah in mind, I imagine Jesus was very excited as he traveled to Jerusalem at the age of twelve on his way to the Passover festival with his family.

When the Passover was over, Mary and Joseph headed home, traveling in a caravan and thinking that Jesus was with their relatives. When they traveled back to Jerusalem looking for Jesus, they found him in the Temple "sitting in the midst of the teachers, both listening to them and asking them questions. And all who heard him were amazed at his understanding and his answers" (vs 46–47).

Why was this time so significant in the life of Jesus? He was about to become a man. He had studied and was ready. Now he was beginning to be recognized for the maturity he was exhibiting. In our American culture, we have no recognizable ceremony or time when a community affirms a boy becoming a man.

The third source of influence is *the church.* For years pastors have taught the biblical view of manhood. However, in the past thirty years there has been a deliberate assault of our modern culture with feminist ideology of gender neutrality. With this constant bombardment, our traditional teachings about masculine roles have been silenced or reinterpreted.

Concerning this dangerous trend in our society, Wall Street Journal columnist Walter Benjamin stated: "As a child, I always accompanied my parents to church after Sunday School. As I looked up at the protective, strong, yet compassionate face of my father, I intuitively knew the church wanted to forge a link between the qualities of God and that of earthly fathers. But have you listened carefully to your church's liturgy recently? If so, God may be referred to as everything except Father. The very idea that calling God "Father" has been harmful to women isn't merely wrong—it's dangerous. The sanitizers are actually destroying a divine measurement that has historically held husbands and their sons responsible."[8]

In a day when men need the support and affirmation of the church, we are relenting to the pressures of society rather than becoming an influence. But why is the lack of a father or at least an active father so devastating to child development?

THE BIOLOGICAL NEED FOR A FATHER IN THE HOME

The answer to the question of why the lack of an active father is so devastating to child development is profound, complicated, and many faceted. The need is first and foremost based on the way God has created us. There has been a natural biological need for human connection

8. Benjamin, *Wall Street*, 3.

since the creation of humanity. This need greatly affects our development and is especially evident in the closest of relationships, the relationship between a child and his father and mother. A great deal of scientific evidence shows that there are numerous biological factors dependent on these close relationships that affect a child's early and adolescent development. The monograph produced by the Commission on Children at Risk, titled *Hardwired to Connect, the New Scientific Case for Authoritative Communities*, proposes that a great deal of scientific evidence strongly shows that "we are hardwired for close attachments to other people, beginning with our mothers, fathers, and extended family, and then moving out to the broader community. The mechanics by which we become and stay attached to others are biologically primed and increasingly discernible in the basic structure of the brain."[9] Allan N. Schore of the UCLA School of Medicine says, "The idea is that we are born to form attachments, that our brains are physically wired to develop in tandem with another's, through emotional communication, beginning before words are spoken."[10] In other words, our very brain structure demands that a healthy, close relationship to immediate family, especially one's father and mother, is absolutely indispensable for proper emotional development.

The monograph continues by stating, "Even as children grow into adolescence, parental presence can have an impact on their biology. Researchers have found that, for an adolescent girl, living in close proximity to her biological father tends to slow down the onset of puberty. Conversely, living with a biologically unrelated adult male—for example, a stepfather or mother's boyfriend—seems to speed up the onset of puberty."[11]

There has been a long debate between the impact of nature versus nurture in the development of children. Do children develop negatively or positively because of genetics or does the influence of one's particular nurturing have a greater influence? Further research has shown that " social environment can change the relationship between a specific gene and the behavior associated with that gene."[12] This new evidence gives us reason to marvel at how wonderfully our created structures interact with our relationships as part of God's design.

9. Commission, *Hardwired*, 14–15.

10. Ibid., 16.

11. Ibid., 18.

12. Ibid., 19.

Finally, the influence of close relationships has a profound influence on the child's development. "The ongoing development of morality in later childhood and adolescence involves the human capacity to idealize individuals and ideas.[13] Our sense of right and wrong originates largely from the biologically-primed need to connect with others. . . . Thwarting the child's need for close attachments to others also thwarts basic moral development."[14] Of course, this moral development will progress in a positive or negative way depending on the type of influence imposed on the child. Even the child's concept of God is closely connected to his relationship with his parents. "Ample research now suggests that children's concepts of God—who God is and how God acts—initially stem partly from the child's actual day-to-day experiences with his parents."[15]

It takes little effort to realize that the absence of the father in the home, complicated by the widespread number of working mothers, has devastated our society. We must do everything possible to train our men to be faithful and consistent fathers and to teach women the importance of mothers staying at home, at least when the children are not in school.

Another essential need for a father's nurturing is that a father is the substance of destiny for the child. What do I mean by that? It is the presence of the father in the home that influences the boy's masculine characteristics and the girl's feminine characteristics. This forges their identity as they look to the future and determines who they look for in a future life partner.

INNATE DESIRES AND NEEDS OF CHILDHOOD

In the "Men's Fraternity" seminar, Robert Lewis teaches five basic things a son or daughter needs from his or her father.[16]

First, *the child needs time with his or her father.* It is when the child spends time with his or her father that the impact of the relationship is at its strongest. Moral character is imparted, the understanding of what a man and father should strive to be like is gained, lifelong memories are added that will serve to draw the father near his child and provide an anchor the child can lean on through life, and affirmation to children of both sexes is imparted, which will bolster their worth.

13. Ibid., 15.
14. Ibid., 26.
15. Ibid., 28.
16. Lewis, *Fraternity*, session 6.

The lack of this valuable time can be illustrated by the upbringing of Jeffrey Dahmer, the man who was convicted of murdering and dismembering seventeen people back in 1992. Two years after he began his sentence of 957 years in prison, he was murdered by a fellow inmate. In a book titled *A Father's Story*, written by Jeffrey's father Lionel Dahmer, the importance of a father's involvement in the lives of his children becomes clear.

In Lionel Dahmer's words, "Jeffrey Dahmer lived a home life of 'domestic conflict' and parental neglect. And so I wasn't there to see him as he began to sink into himself. I wasn't there to sense that he might be drifting toward that unimaginable realm of fantasy and isolation that it would take nearly thirty years to recognize."[17]

In Deuteronomy 6:6–7 we are given these instructions, "These words, which I am commanding you today, shall be on your heart. You shall teach them diligently to your sons and shall talk of them when you sit in your house and when you walk by the way and when you lie down and when you rise up." In order for parents to commit the time necessary to obey this command to teach their children "when you sit in your house, when you walk by the way, when you lie down, and when you rise up," parents need to spend time with their children. This teaching goes far beyond instruction, it includes life example as well, which can only be exhibited as the parents spend time with their children.

Second, *a child needs life skills*. The well-known verse in Proverbs 22:6 gives parents wise instruction on how to raise their children. This verse exhorts parents to, "Train up a child in the way he should go, even when he is old he will not depart from it." This verse can be interpreted in two ways; both interpretations, I believe, are instructive.

The first interpretation of the phrase "Train up a child in the way he should go" according to commentator Albert Barns, can be correctly interpreted, "The way he should go—or, according to the tenor of his way, i.e., the path especially belonging to, especially fitted for, the individual's character. The proverb enjoins the closest possible study of each child's temperament and the adaptation of "his way of life" to that."[18] This interpretation instructs the parent to understand their child's "bent," abilities, talents, and interests and to nurture these qualities so that he takes them into his future as life practices.

17. Dahmer, *Father's*, 60.

18. Barnes, *Notes*, Prov 22:6.

In his book *Raising a Modern-Day Knight*, Robert Lewis shares the experience one man recorded in a letter. He says: "My Dad tried to teach me how to play baseball when I was a kid, but I was never interested in sports. This made him real mad. I could feel his constant displeasure over this. I later got real interested in electronics, but he wasn't any more interested in that than I was in baseball. At my request, he would take me to an electronics store on Saturday and drop me off for a few hours, but that's about as far as our interaction went."[19]

One of the things a child needs is for the parent to help him understand his life skills so that as a teen or young adult he can plan his life with a career in mind that utilizes these abilities.

According to commentators John Walvoord and Roy Zuck, the second interpretation hinges on the meaning of the word "way." "Since 'way' in Proverbs does not mean personality or stage in life, it is preferable to say that 'way' means *proper* way . . . behavior pattern or godly lifestyle,"[20] ensuring that if trained properly, he will not depart from that lifestyle. "The Hebrew word for 'train' means to dedicate. It is used for dedicating a house (Deut 20:5) and the temple (1 Kgs 8:63; 2 Chr 7:5)."[21] One would expect a parent to dedicate a child to wise godly living rather than to dedicate the child's innate personality practices, as in the first interpretation.

The problem is that many parents that claim Proverbs 22:6 with the previous interpretation are baffled by the way their adult children are living. But as we look at the parenting styles used to raise their children, we will usually find they were parents who, though sometimes faithful in taking their children to church, have neglected to provide the nurturing and modeling required by God. The average Christian parents send their children off to daycare or public school while they both work away from the home leaving little time for serious child rearing. They have relegated their responsibility to others yet claim Proverbs 22:6. I think God requires more from us as parents than that.

The child needs these godly character qualities so he will be equipped to face a life with many temptations and influences. One of the alarming characteristics of our modern society is that many adults do not possess the positive attributes that were once common. A while back a contractor shared with me the difficulty of finding honest and trustworthy employees. He said that, if necessary, he could teach them to read but he could never

19. Lewis, *Knight*, 75.

20. Walvoord, *Knowledge*, Prov 22:6.

21. Ibid.

teach them integrity. He cannot survive as a contractor if his employees steal from his clients or perform substandard work. We need to train our children to have godly qualities of integrity as well as a good work ethic, reliability, respect for others, humility, sexual purity, and control of their tongue. No school class on character development will ever replace what can only be effectively taught in the home.

Third, *a child needs answers to his why questions*. One of the classic passages that challenges parents as they instruct their children is found in the passage discussed earlier, Deuteronomy 6:1–9. The content of the instruction in this passage is the Law or the Word of God, which is taught not so much through family devotions as through lifestyle.

The primary lifestyle-teaching tool that wise parents capitalize on is utilizing teachable moments. These moments when a child is asking a question, and has been impacted by an event or after discipline, are prime opportunities to teach character and to help the child learn and understand. These answers should always be explained from a biblical framework. The child needs to learn that our standard for authority is God's Word.

Equally important is the lifestyle-teaching tool that comes from the practice of consistent discipline. Effective discipline of children includes four basic steps:

1 Never discipline children out of anger, and as much as is possible, measure the discipline by the severity of the offense. In other words, discipline with stronger consequences should be reserved for greater negative behavior. These more severe offenses usually include behaviors that are moral in nature; such as lying, defiance of authority, disrespect of parents, or cruelty to another person.

2. After the child has finished weeping (which for many is a normal response to discipline), it is wise for the parent administering the discipline to take the child onto his lap and ask several questions in order to discern if the child fully understands why he was disciplined. If the child doesn't fully understand, the parent has a wonderful teachable moment to explain the offense that was committed. It is important to make sure the child understands that the authority did not come solely from Mommy or Daddy, an "I told you so!" response. On the contrary, it is because God says so. As such, explain what God says about the offense from his Word. Help the child understand that life's

practices need to conform to God's will not just our demands. This is necessary in order to help the child develop biblical convictions and not just compliance to parental authority.

3. If the child is a believer in Christ, it is important to explain that there was also an offense made to God that must be confessed to him as well (1 John 1:9).
4. After reconciliation, the parent should affirm their love. Tell the child that Mommy or Daddy still loves him and that there is nothing they can do that would ever take away that love. The parent could then end the discipline with a big hug. Children need the assurance and security that comes from full reconciliation.

A fourth innate need a child has is for *convictions imparted from the father's example.* These convictions form a code of conduct, a foundation of behavioral practices providing a compass for one's entire life. This code of conduct becomes even more crucial when you consider the immoral character of modern society. For example, the seven greatest problems reported by schools in 1940 were:

1. Talking out of turn
2. Chewing gum
3. Making noise
4. Running in the halls
5. Cutting in line
6. Violating the dress code
7. Littering

Fifty years later the seven greatest problems reported by schools were:

1. Drug abuse
2. Alcohol abuse
3. Pregnancy
4. Suicide
5. Rape
6. Robbery
7. Assault[22]

22. Morrison, lecture, np.

The greatest way a father can teach godly character qualities is to leave a godly example. Have you ever noticed that when a sexually risqué image comes on the television screen an adolescent son or daughter looks to see how Dad responds? They are looking for his example. It doesn't matter whether the father's life is godly or carnal, a child will look to him as a model. A good role model also increases the value of the final important tool in establishing positive character qualities.

On three different occasions the Apostle Paul exhorted his followers to be a model or example for others to follow. In 1 Timothy 4:12, he said, "Let no one look down on your youthfulness, but rather in speech, conduct, love, faith and purity, show yourself an example of those who believe." (see also 2 Thess 3:9 and Heb 13:7). How much more should we as parents provide that example for our children to follow?

Fifth, *a child needs words of affirmation.* Comments like "I am so proud of you," "You sure are growing up to be a fine young man or lady," "I love you," and "You're a good boy or girl." We tend to be negative and overly critical. It has been said that it takes seven positive comments to make up for every negative criticism. Positive words of praise go a long way in reinforcing proper behavior. They motivate children to act and live in a way pleasing to his parents. Words of affirmation also increase the bond between parent and child and widen the door of communication.

Proverbs 17:6 tell us that "Grandchildren are the crown of old men, and the glory of sons is their fathers." I have twelve Grandchildren and every Thursday we have Grandpa/Grandma Day when we spend several hours with our Grandchildren. I look forward to these days because my Grandchildren are my crown. As Brown states, "The Hebrew word translated 'glory' in Proverbs 17:6 is *thephara*. The basic idea is 'beauty' or 'glory' but in this particular instance *thephara* refers to the act of 'boasting.'"[23] Just as Grandchildren are the crown of their Grandparents so sons have great regard and delight for their fathers even to the point that they desire to boast about them. Boys don't brag about their mother but they will tell their friends that their father is stronger. This desire on the part of sons is innate, not learned. It is the natural, God-given desire on the part of boys to look up to their father and they crave their father's approval and words of affirmation.

23. Brown, *Lexicon*, 802.

THE SCARS LEFT BY AN ABSENT FATHER ALSO IMPACT FEMALE CHILDREN

According to Charles Lewis, when Dad is not present or is distant, the young lady develops a personality with one of two flaws. Either the young lady becomes insecure and anxious, having difficulty forming healthy relationships with men, or she may become inappropriately self-assertive, angry, and promiscuous. He goes on to say that one common historical trait of most of the radical feminists of the sixties is that they had abusive fathers.

If Dad is present during the developmental years, the young lady becomes very secure in her identity as a woman and is able to relate to the opposite sex and enjoy a highly fulfilling sex life with her husband. In other words, the young lady's admiration for and trust in a man comes from a relationship with her father.[24]

In our modern society, Western culture encourages and even expects that the modern woman seeks a career and at the same time belittles any desire to stay at home raising children. This is even celebrated and encouraged by the new holiday, "Take Your Daughter to Work Day." The persistent effort is to demonize traditional feminine values in favor of being assertive, sexy, and dominate. After spending a number of years in a career, many women actually live in fear of becoming a wife and mother. We should encourage young mothers to seek counsel, even the mentoring of mature godly older women. As instructed in Titus 2:3–5, "Older women likewise are to be reverent in their behavior, not malicious gossips nor enslaved to much wine, teaching what is good, so that they may encourage the young women to love their husbands, to love their children, to be sensible, pure, workers at home, kind, being subject to their own husbands, so that the word of God will not be dishonored."

What can we do to encourage young ladies to pursue careers as stay-at-home moms? First, we need to provide a healthy home environment with an active and loving father and a committed stay-at-home mom. Each parent needs to follow biblical roles and demonstrate a loving relationship as husband and wife. Secondly, it is important that we affirm the high calling for a woman to raise the next generation of children. Nurturing takes time, and it cannot be done effectively with what little strength a mother has after a full day at the workplace.

24. Lewis, *Fraternity,* session 23.

In our home we held this pursuit as a high and rewarding calling. We were willing to sacrifice material things for the privilege and responsibility of my wife building a career as a stay-at-home mom. That meant we had to manage our money well, and it was necessary that we stayed out of debt. God has blessed our efforts; all four of our children grew up with a strong Christian character, and each one is active in serving the Lord. Because of the positive impact this has had on their lives, each of our children shares the priority of the wife in their family staying at home and enjoying the same blessing.

HEALING THE WOUND CAUSED BY AN ABSENTEE FATHER

If you have been an absentee father and desire for the wound to be healed in your son or daughter, you must *seek reconciliation and healing.* God sincerely wants reconciliation between the father and his children. It was so important that he concluded the very last verse in the Old Testament with Malachi 4:6, "He (Elijah) will restore the hearts of the fathers to their children and the hearts of the children to their fathers, so that I will not come and smite the land with a curse." I would like to recommend four steps that need to be followed in securing this vitally important reconciliation.

First, begin praying for your son or daughter on a regular basis. Pray that God will make it possible for reconciliation.

Second, meet with your son or daughter face-to-face and ask him or her to forgive you. Admit that nothing can adequately make up for the time lost and the mistakes made but if he or she will forgive, you would like to try to become the father they never had. Don't give up if he or she does not receive your gesture. Because the wounds are deep, the son or daughter may need time to think about your proposal. Pray for healing on a regular basis and be persistent with your effort.

Third, begin spending time with your son or daughter. Allow them to vent without becoming defensive and answer the "why" questions to the best of your ability without trying to make excuses.

Fourth, if your son or daughter is ready to receive it, begin to give honest and sincere words of affirmation. Tell him or her that you love them and that you are proud of them. Praise them for accomplishments no matter how small.

If you were wounded by an absentee father, *seek personal healing.* First, choose to forgive your father for the many hurts and offenses he caused. Even if your father is deceased or even if he has not acknowledged the wrong he has committed, choose to forgive. In Matthew 6:14–15, Jesus said, "For if you forgive others for their transgressions, your heavenly Father will also forgive you. But if you do not forgive others, then your Father will not forgive your transgressions." He never said to forgive if the offender has apologized to you. You should forgive even if the offense was never acknowledged. This may be difficult but God will enable you.

To "forgive and forget" is never possible. We don't have the capacity to push the delete button as on a computer. As you forgive, the memories will retreat and you will think of the offense less and less. Also, we must not evaluate whether or not we have forgiven based on the amount of pain we are suffering. Pain will subside over time as we forgive. To forgive is to decide not to hold the person accountable for wrong done. Leave the need for justice in God's hands. Romans 12:19 says, "Never take your own revenge, beloved, but leave room for the wrath of God, for it is written, 'Vengeance is mine, I will repay,' says the Lord." When we refuse to forgive, resentment builds, and resentment turns to bitterness. Bitterness hurts no one but the one with the resentment.

Second, begin to pray for your father and that God will provide reconciliation. Don't give up quickly but persevere even if it takes time. One day you will be glad you tried, even if you are unsuccessful.

Third, courageously seek reconciliation. Don't wait for him to initiate or for the circumstances to be perfect. Seek God's direction and the right timing. With much prayer, God will work in his heart preparing him for your meeting.

Fourth, if you have caused any hurt or conflict in your relationship, resolve to apologize and seek forgiveness from your father for the offense you are guilty of.

Fifth, ask your father if he would be willing to work with you to grow your relationship.

Sixth, tell your father that you love him, and if he doesn't respond back to you with an expression of love, convey that you hope that he will grow in his love for you.

Seventh, ask your father to give you his blessing. Whether your father is a believer or not, God will respond to a request for a blessing from him because of his position as father. Remember that if your father is still alive, time is fleeting. You will not always have this opportunity and the available time is narrowing.

Eighth, resolve not to make the same mistakes with your children. Make plans and set goals that will insure your success. God will help you become a good father or mother even though you did not have a good model to follow.

One of the problems with a man or woman who grew up with a distant or nonexistent father is an additional wound that is entirely different. This is a wound from the mother.

THE WOUND CAUSED BY BEING OVERLY BONDED WITH THE MOTHER

Other than the father, no one has the life-changing influence on every aspect of children's lives like the mother does. The way she interacts with her children during their growing up years has an unparalleled influence on their self-image, career choice, personality, and even their marriage.

All mothers intend to have a good influence on their children. However, in the absence of a father or where there is a father who was non-functional or distant, the mother is forced to take leadership and to become the dominant force in the upbringing of her children. This dominance produces its own set of problems for the children.

At birth, there is a physical cutting or separation made when the umbilical cord is cut. Likewise, there needs to be a gradual cutting of the emotional umbilical cord as the child grows. When there is no functional father in the home, this emotional cord is often left intact. In Genesis 2:24, man is exhorted: "For this reason a man shall leave his father and his mother, and be joined to his wife; and they shall become one flesh." The physical and emotional union being dissolved, the man is now commanded to have the physical and emotional union or oneness with his wife. When both the severing and new union does not occur, there are problems in the marriage.

This wound caused by being overly bonded with the mother is much different than the wound caused by the absentee father. It is not a wound of abuse, neglect, and absenteeism but a wound that is subtler and is disguised by love, care, and over-attention. Even though this wound looks like love, it actually manifests itself by control and begins to warp the boy's masculine psyche and the girl's concept of what a woman should be like.

One may ask how this wound could have occurred in the first place. With the absence of a father, mothers may respond in one of four different ways:

First, a mother may be ignorant of the damage she is causing her children. She may not understand that her children, especially her sons, need to develop a healthy separation. Many boys grow up feeling that their masculinity is suffocated.

Second, a mother in this circumstance is often a single mom experiencing her own struggles and emotional pain. She is needy and has no way to fill this need. Sometimes the son, especially as he grows older, takes the place of a husband, in a limited sense.

The third characteristic of a mother in this situation is an unwillingness to release control. Because her husband didn't provide leadership, it became necessary for her to exert control. Often, when the husband does not meet his responsibilities as leader of the home, it is due to the loss of respect for his wife because she developed divided loyalties between his children and him.

The fourth response is when a mother tries to fill in the gap. Instead of finding surrogate fathers from relatives or friends, she seeks to become both father and mother to her children. This is both stressful for her and damaging to both male and female children.

As the young man grows up and falls in love, he may respond in one of two ways. First, he may become submissive to his prospective wife just as he did to his mother. During the engagement period his fiancé sees this as a loving, sensitive, and considerate quality. It seems like he always puts her first, wanting her to decide and to do what she desires. This becomes endearing to her until they are married. After a few months of marriage, the wife begins wanting her husband to begin taking the lead. She may even begin to nag him, causing conflict in the marriage. When he was dating her, his ideal was to find a "mother wife" because that's all he knew. Now he begins to feel resentful of his wife's nagging and finds it hard to make this drastic personality change of becoming assertive.

The other way the young man may respond is to feel threatened by the assertiveness of his new wife, causing him to be overly dominant, demanding, and controlling in order to win his freedom from the dominance he felt from his mother. The outcome could result in his being physically and verbally abusive.

The daughter is unknowingly mentored to become a more assertive person and to manifest these qualities later on in marriage, while her new husband will likely resist her assertiveness.

One of the classic examples of this far too common syndrome is the TV sitcom *Everybody Loves Raymond*. The character Ray Barone and his brother Robert were raised by an assertive and manipulative mother. The father was distant and uninvolved in the upbringing of their children. Ray then marries Debra who he expects to fit the bill as a "mother wife." The sitcom continues episode after episode with the mother manipulating everyone, her boys competing for their mother's love, and everyone lying so as not to face the wrath of their manipulative mother. At the same time, Ray's wife wants him to be more involved with his children and to take leadership, which he constantly avoids by making excuses and rationalizing. Nevertheless, she continues to nag and pressure him to be a better father.

In my ministry I see the previous scenarios over and over in the counseling room. As our society continues to deteriorate, these problems will become even more common. It is possible for these assertive and non-assertive people to change but these kinds of changes take time. Unfortunately, most couples don't have the patience and opt for the easier solution of divorce.

Our number one childrearing problem in American society is not the poor quality of our public education but the deterioration of the family. This is compounded in the urban environment and it begins with the absent father. We need to teach our men to be leaders and to understand their indispensable role in the family. Unfortunately, in our twenty-first century society, we not only have absentee fathers but, with two-career households, the problem is multiplied with the absentee mother. The poor children are left to be raised by the nanny, daycare, traditional grade school, after-school programs, babysitters, or just to fend for themselves. Having to function as both father and mother, the single mom is forced to become very dominate as she tries to hold things together and function with some sense of efficiency. This creates its own type of wound as the children live under a mother who is dominate, protective, and often very attached. The current generation will carry even greater wounds as they enter adulthood.

What are some solutions for those who have the wound caused by being overly bonded with mother? First, it is necessary for men to break this over-involvement with the mother in their lives. You need to stand up to her and make those hard choices of independence. It is necessary to choose what is best for your family, even if you get opposition from your mother. Examples of this include when decisions need to be made about where you spend Thanksgiving or Christmas and whose house you stay in when you are in town. Also, to allow the bad influence and incompatible childrearing styles by parents as they babysit is both destructive for your children and damaging for your marriage relationship. Come to grips with the understanding that breaking your mom's over-involvement and no longer allowing her manipulation and dominance to continue is both good for her as well as you. To properly lead your home is impossible without this break.

Second, recognize that your ultimate goal is to become a man whose vision is fixed on what God thinks and not on what your mom thinks. In Matthew 10:37, Jesus said, "He who loves father or mother more than Me is not worthy of Me."

Third, get support, encouragement, and help from other men or from a counselor and develop a plan of healthy independence from your mom. This plan should address specific issues that cause continued trouble along with a plan of action. This plan should include boundaries for how you will interact in the future. Evaluate the boundaries by asking test questions such as: Is the boundary clear? Is the boundary too tight? Is it too loose? Does the boundary continue to honor my mom, and is it fair?

The plan should also include clear consequences that will be enacted when the boundaries are violated. The plan rises and falls on the consistent follow-through with these consequences. Communicate your plan to your mother face-to-face or by letter, and begin following it regardless to how she responds. She may respond with anger or withdrawal, but in time she will adjust if you are lovingly firm, consistent, and continue to persevere.

After you develop your plan, you must apologize to your wife for not correcting the problem sooner and ask for her support and prayers. Ask her not to get involved. It is vital that all interaction and communication with your mother come from you and not from your wife.

The natural reaction to the problems of our families, which directly influence and dictate the plight of our cities and our nation, radiates a sense of hopelessness. I need to emphasize here that there is amazing hope in Jesus Christ. Through God's redemptive work, through believers who are God's ambassadors coming alongside the fatherless, and by our involvement in discipleship, counseling, love, acceptance, emotional support, and being a model to follow, we can help men and women make the difficult adjustments and prevent serious marital problems. With perseverance and consistency there can be real healing and help. How can we help people with such great needs? One person at a time. Instead of despairing with a sense of hopelessness, we must roll up our sleeves and, with God's power and guidance, become part of the solution.

REVIEW QUESTIONS

1. According to statistics, what are the negative effects of the absence of a father in the home and how does the absence of a father in the home affect a child's worldview?
2. What does the scientific biological evidence indicate about the way our brain is hardwired?
3. According to the author, what are five innate desires and needs each child possesses?
4. How does the absence of a father impact female children?
5. Because of the absence of a husband, what are the four different ways the mother is apt to respond?
6. What are the two possible ways a man who was overly bonded with his mother is apt to respond in his own marriage?

10

Living in the City

Achieving Unbounded Success in a Degraded Environment

WHEN WE CONSIDERED MOVING to the inner city of Chicago twenty-nine years ago, we faced many reasons to go elsewhere. At that time we had three children, another to be born two years later. We had heard a lot about crime, gangs, and drugs. Would our family be safe? We knew the cost of living was higher in large cities than many other places we could live. Could we afford the costs, especially on a missionary income? We had heard that the education in the public schools was poor in the inner city. What would we do to insure that our children received a good and safe education? Would they be negatively influenced by the corruption and permissiveness so pervasive in the city? We would be living in Chicago's Humboldt Park, which one gang expert from a nearby university had written was one of the worst gang neighborhoods in the entire nation. These and other concerns plagued us as we prayed and sought counsel. Many Christian friends warned us that we should not expose our children to that environment. After all, "there are people everywhere who need Christ."

As we struggled through our decision, I reflected on my theology of God. I knew that God is all-powerful and that he knows all things, even the future. I affirmed that God is a good God and that he is my Lord. I was reminded that God is able and will protect his own who live obediently according to his will. It is easy to believe intellectually in what the Bible says about God. It is another thing to hang our lives and the lives of our loved ones on it, to really believe it.

There were, and are, many men and women who have chosen not to come to the city to live and serve because of the previously mentioned reasons. I have learned that many have not let their theology guide their lives. I knew I had to trust our good God who is also the sustainer of all things. As I struggled and prayed, God brought a truth to my heart. He impressed upon me that the safest place in the entire world is in the center of God's will and the most dangerous place is outside of his will. We could move to Chicago with full confidence in God and live in peace. Though we needed to use wisdom and common sense, we could live without being afraid. Our God would be with us.

Now, as I look back over the past twenty-nine years, I can testify of many things we have seen, some terrible indeed. But God has put a hedge of protection around my family. My children, my wife, and I have never been injured, and our house has never been broken into. Yes, we have had some close calls, and God does allow trials in our lives, some of which may at times be perpetrated by ungodly people. But I am convinced that nothing can happen unless our good God in his wisdom allows it to happen. He is with us, and he will always help us through the most desperate of circumstances. Today all my children are grown up. They are men and women of character, serving the Lord in the inner city.

But it is true that there are difficulties and adjustments living in the city. Many committed servants of God come here totally unprepared to face these challenges, and some of their ministries fail. In this chapter I would like to share how God has helped us cope while living in a hostile environment. If God has called you to the city, he will guide your child rearing so you will be "Achieving Unbounded Success in a Degraded Environment."

IS THERE ANYTHING GOOD ABOUT LIVING IN THE CITY?

Before I outline the negative elements and share advice for living in an urban environment, I would like to note that there is an abundance of good things the city has to offer.

Large cities provide an abundance of cultural, educational, and entertainment opportunities. Large cities are saturated with all types of large and small museums, theaters, operas, symphonic orchestras, and hundreds of restaurants with every ethnic food imaginable. Many come to the large cities for shopping, with hundreds of stores of every type to choose from. Professional sports teams compete in every large city for spectators to enjoy football, basketball, baseball, soccer, hockey, as well as high school and college level sports events.

In Chicago we have thirty miles of shoreline along Lake Michigan. Scattered along the shoreline on the east side of the city are numerous beaches providing opportunities for swimming, fishing, hiking, roller-blading, and biking. Looking west from the waterfront you can see the beautiful downtown Chicago landscape, one of the most beautiful in the world. On the western side of the city we have thirty miles of forest preserves, which provide large picnic areas and miles and miles of paved trails for hiking and biking.

Parks are plentiful, though are not as abundant as needed, especially in the inner-city areas. Even so, there are many parks and many of them very large. The park department provides swimming pools, supervised summer activities, and team sports for children, teens, and adults, as well as classes that teach swimming, gymnastics, crafts, and aerobics, to name a few.

Large cities provide many scheduled events. In Chicago we have over fifty events scheduled throughout the summer. Some events are large while others are specialized; some are citywide events while others are provided for neighborhoods and ethnic interests. The city plays host to many parades, celebrations, and even several farmers markets. Some events are large attractions like the Air and Water Show, The Taste of Chicago, and Independence Day Fireworks, each attracting five hundred thousand to several millions of people per event. There are also many other popular festivals like the Gospel Fest, Blues Fest, and Country Music Fest. Many types of nationally known music entertainers and concerts are scheduled throughout the year. Large urban areas also attract many conventions, as well as secular and Christian conferences and seminars that are helpful and convenient as we develop our ability to minister more effectively.

One of the advantages of living in a large city is the plethora of colleges, universities, and technical schools both secular and religious. There are also many opportunities for continuing and specialized education that do not require college acceptance.

Hospitals and medical centers are abundant in cities, including some of the world's renowned university medical centers and research institu-

tions. The number and variety of hospitals is one of the advantages, but this variety provides a challenge for the minister who visits parishioners. Unlike some churches that may have several people at the same hospital at once, we visit in over thirty hospitals and sometimes have people in four or five different hospitals at the same time.

The availability of various modes of transportation is also a great advantage of large cities. Because of the availability of city buses and subway trains along with regional bus and train service, many people in the city get along fine without ever owning an automobile. Most large cities also have one or more international airports, train stations, and bus depots. Often when we go to the airport or take care of business downtown, it is more convenient to take the subway or bus, avoiding the traffic and expense of parking.

Television and radio stations are abundant. They usually provide a clear reception so that many find it unnecessary to purchase cable or a satellite dish.

For those with a burden of reaching people for the kingdom of God, the city provides masses of people along with every ethnic group imaginable. The world is living at our doorstep. These people are often more receptive to the gospel than they would be in their homeland. For no other reason, the great potential for changing people's lives is by itself motive for many who desire to make an eternal impact, to move to the urban setting.

As you can see, there are many advantages and blessings awaiting those who move to the city. God loves the city because God loves mankind. When we look at the city with what it has to offer—and understand God's provision, protection, and help—the blessings far outweigh the disadvantages.

WHERE SHOULD I LIVE?

I believe some have made a serious mistake serving in a "bad" neighborhood and choosing to live elsewhere, perhaps in a nicer part of town or even commuting from the suburbs where crime is not as severe. In the chapter titled "Principles of Urban Ministry, Part 1," as I explained "incarnational ministry," I reviewed how Jesus moved into the worst neighborhood. He would live as one of the people even though they would become very hostile to him. I believe that in order to be effective and to maintain credibility with the people we are trying to reach, it is imperative that we live among them. We truly can trust God for our protection.

When we moved to Chicago, God led us to purchase a house only two blocks from where we were ministering. We desired to have a place with a large yard where our children could play. Large yards are at a premium and are usually expensive in the city. One day, shortly after we moved in, a realtor came to our door and asked me if we would be interested in buying the vacant lot next to our house. In our neighborhood, a lot is about 25 feet wide by 115 feet deep. The city had confiscated it because the owner had not paid his property taxes. He said the city wanted $1,500 for the property. At that time we were living on missionary support and had no savings. When I told the realtor that I had no money, he encouraged me to submit a small offer for the purchase of the lot. We agreed to pay $500, which the city subsequently turned down because the offer, they said, was too low. A month later they contacted me agreeing to sell the property to us for our original offer. Five hundred dollars may not seem much to most people, but in 1985, for a poor missionary, it was far more then we could afford.

On that Thursday afternoon it looked unlikely that we could come up with the money by the Monday deadline. As I went to work the next morning I was notified that a man who had heard me speak at a Missionary Conference was wondering if we had any needs that he could help with by providing a special financial gift. When I told the director of my need for $500 to purchase the vacant lot, he encouraged me to expand my list including other needs. In order to make the new addition of property usable, it would be necessary to add topsoil so I could plant a lawn and install additional fencing to surround my expanded property. We were also desirous of purchasing a used piano needed for my children to take lessons. The entire need list came to a total of $1,800. By the Monday morning deadline, I had in my hands a check for $1,800. God had given us the large yard we desired. Psalms 37:4 says, "Delight yourself in the LORD; and he will give you the desires of your heart." God proved his Word true. God had provided not a need but something we wanted. He is indeed a good God.

If you live in obedience to God's will, you can be assured he will provide your every need and sometimes even your wants. He can even make a negative living condition something you are comfortable with; yes, you may even learn to like it.

COPING WITH SAFETY

The bottom line with safety is our dependence on and trust in our God who can protect us. We learn to put our confidence in our faithful God and to live in peace and assurance. I believe this truth is foundational; nevertheless, God expects us to live a wise life exercising common sense. What are some practices we can implement to make our environment a safe place to live?

Prepare your home so that it is difficult to break into. If your apartment is in the basement or on the first floor, windows should be protected with security bars. If you are on the second or third floor, it is necessary to make sure that back porches and staircases have secure windows. The doors should also have deadbolts on each outside entrance, and many people have security alarms installed. If you do not have bars on the unsecured windows as listed above, it is important that you not leave those windows open, especially at night or when you are out. Most second or third floor windows are safe for air conditioners or for leaving the windows open even without bars because of the difficulty for intruders to access them.

Take frequent walks in your neighborhood, making casual acquaintance with as many people as possible. People are more apt to help those they know. Likewise, some intruders will not be as apt to break into your home because they know you. Becoming friendly with people in your neighborhood also makes it possible for you to be a witness. We looked for opportunities to serve our neighbors, taking cookies or other baked goods to their homes, pushing their cars out of the snow when stuck, and sometimes watching over their homes when they are gone, and they do the same for us. In our block we became known as "those church people," which provided for us a level of respect even by many gang members.

Because of the proliferation of crime, many have joined or even organized a neighborhood watch. This is a system in which participating neighbors keep a lookout for each other. If someone appears to be doing something that is suspicious, the neighbor calls the police and the next person on his phone chain. Each succeeding person calls the police and the next person. Multiple calls provide a quick response.

Often we drove our kids to activities. Our children didn't walk out of our immediate area, and we made a rule in our home that nobody went away from home after dark unless they were picked up and taken home by a trustworthy person. There was no hanging out in the neighborhood after dark unless they were in our own yard. Our kids were instructed to never go inside a person's home without permission. If our teenagers found themselves in a rare situation requiring a walk or bike ride after dark, and if they were unable to call us, we instructed them to always stay on main, well-lit streets.

We maintained an interest in who our kids hung out with, making sure they had Christian friends. This will be harder if you move to the city with teenagers who may not be willing to comply with a stricter set of guidelines.

My wife learned that it was better to carry a purse with a thick strap put over her head and not just hung on her shoulder. Women should never set their purses on the seat next to them in a bus or subway or even in a grocery cart. A loose purse is easy for someone to grab and then run out of the door. We never carried much money, and I learned that in a crowd it was a good idea to put my billfold in my front pant's pocket.

In a large city you can never leave things, even of modest value, visible in the car. A friend's window was knocked out as the thief stole an inexpensive sleeping bag. Another had his car battery stolen when he left the door unlocked. It is also wise to chain outdoor items like a grill or lawn furniture to the fence, especially if you have a low fence that is easy to climb over.

All door-to-door visitations should be done in pairs. No one should go to a concealed back door even if there is a note on the front door directing one to the back, unless, of course, it is a friend's home.

Some people move to the inner city and live in fear of gangs. As a minister in the city I learned that I should not be afraid. The Apostle John said, "Greater is he who is in you than he who is in the world" (1 John 4:4). I need to be wise in how I conduct myself but I have never lived in fear. Some are also concerned with the abundance of drugs, which are very easy to obtain in the city. They fear that the pressure of peer drug use would be a threatening influence on their teenagers. I do not believe that this needs to be a problem for committed believers who truly raise their children in the nurture and admonition of the Lord. If parents maintain consistent and loving discipline, spend adequate time with their children, and provide godly examples, God will provide the needed help and protection. You should not have to fear that you are sacrificing your children to the streets. You can trust God that your children will not end up in gangs or as drug addicts.

Even though this list may seem frightening, we must not live in fear. God is with us but he does not want us to be foolish. Therefore, we should do all we can to insure safety and, at the same time, trust our faithful God.

COPING WITH THE ENVIRONMENT

One of the difficulties in moving into an urban area, especially if you have never lived in a large city, is the difference in culture. Many people actually experience a type of cultural shock. It can take months before one begins to feel at home with the differences.

With the well-lit streets in the city, it is never totally dark. One who has been raised in a rural area may find it difficult to adjust. I installed black-out shades on my bedroom windows so I could block out the night light even from the back of the house with our lit alleys and our neighbor's outdoor security spotlights.

The city is nocturnal; it never goes to sleep. There are people on the sidewalks and cars traveling residential streets all night long. With activity comes noise. In the front of the house you may hear the loud noise from the amplified car sound system or stereo player at the neighbor's house who has his door and windows wide open. Sometimes a portable stereo unit is brought outside. In the back of the house is the alley with cars passing through or people talking. I should also not overlook mentioning the parties that can go on late into the night, especially on the summer weekends. Little concern is exercised by those making the noise that someone may be sleeping. It was a big help to us when we installed central air-conditioning and were able to keep our windows closed. When all else failed, we found it necessary to turn on our own music in order to drown out the noise.

Moreover, many people find it hard to get used to the dirty environment of the city. Neighborhood litter is something one has to accept. Chicago, however, is not as bad as some cities, with our street cleaning trucks going down each street once a month. Even so, I find it necessary to clean up the litter on a regular basis that blows into my yard.

Many city neighborhoods are plagued with graffiti, much of it sprayed as street gang tags. Since graffiti breeds more graffiti, the only way to fight it on your property is to immediately clean it off or paint over it, otherwise it will multiply. A number of years ago our city purchased twenty-five Graffiti Buster trucks armed with high-pressure sprayers blasting a water and baking soda mixture. This has been very effective cleaning the graffiti off the buildings and viaducts. Along with these cleaning units, the city banned the sale of spray paint cans in the city limits. This two-pronged approach has made it possible for our city to control graffiti proliferation, making a big improvement in our city's appearance.

In the inner city, especially in African-American and Hispanic communities, people spend more time outside. The sidewalks are busy and many front yards and porches are crowded with people. It is not uncommon to see ten to fifteen people in front of a house hanging out. There are people sitting on a stoop or chair talking with family members and neighbors. It is good to go out and meet people, to become part of the neighborhood. Often teens will play basketball or football right in the street, moving out of the way to let cars pass. The reason streets have become the playground is because there is a shortage of tennis courts, baseball diamonds, football fields, and basketball courts, especially in inner city communities. Even parks are often farther away and fewer per capita in the city. This fosters idleness, and idleness breeds vandalism and petty crime. Because there is a lack of play space, we purchased the extra city lot, as mentioned above, doubling the size of our property. It became an oasis in our neighborhood, a place where our kids and their friends could come to play basketball and football. We wanted our children to play at their own home, not away from home where we would lose the ability of supervision.

Another factor that is hard for some to adjust to is traffic congestion common in the city. "Rush hour" is a misnomer because traffic is heavy all day with certain periods slightly lighter. The best way to deal with street congestion is to accept it. If you have a negative, intolerant attitude about the traffic, you will never learn to be content in the city. Second, we try to travel as much as possible late morning, early to mid-afternoon, or evening when the traffic is not as busy. Third, we often take a bus or subway, especially when going downtown.

Another common practice in the city that may be difficult to get used to is street solicitation. I am asked almost daily for change from sidewalk solicitors and those working the stoplight intersections. Often at intersections the person carries a sign indicating that he is a war veteran or that he is homeless. Sometimes the reason for the request is persuasive. For example, I have been approached by people asking for money for a bus or subway ticket to get to work because they left their wallet at home. One man asked me for a dollar to buy a bus ticket to get to a doctor's appointment. When I told him that I would buy him a bus ticket, he conveniently noticed a friend who would drive him there. He obviously didn't want the ticket but the money. A lady asked for money to buy milk for her baby. I told her I would buy her some milk. She then told me that her baby was lactose intolerant and needed goat's milk, which they didn't sell in the immediate area, and that if I would give her the money she could buy some. From years of experience, I strongly encourage you not to give out money to people you do not know. Usually the money will go for the purchase of drugs or alcohol. When I was new in the city, I would give solicitors money and watch where they went. Sometimes I would drive around the block or stand out of sight to see if they did indeed get on the subway or go into the fast-food restaurant. They almost always walked into a bar or the liquor store. When people say they are hungry and ask for money, I often take them into a restaurant and purchase a meal for them. I have also bought bus tickets for people but I never give out money to strangers. I believe many well-meaning Christians only become enablers when they give out cash to street solicitors. God expects us to be good stewards with the money he has given us.

How then can we help those who have an obvious need? I have taken many people to drug and alcohol rehab centers or to a hospital detox ward. At church we have lists of shelters we can direct them to and have developed a food pantry for those in need as well as a listing of other food pantries in the area, though a caution that must be considered is that patrons of food pantries sometimes sell the food for drugs. As such, we limit the amount we give out and allow them to come only once each day we are open.

At Thanksgiving we distribute food baskets and frozen turkeys. For some people we have even cooked the turkey in advance because we knew the person would sell the frozen turkey for drug money. At Christmas time we organize parties for needy children where we provide gifts. Sometimes we allow the children to open their gift and play with it so the parents will be unable to sell their toy. I realize that all of this may sound like we are overly cautious, but we have found that it is important to know the people we are trying to minister to and, when necessary, to take wise precautions so as not to be an enabler.

COPING WITH A POOR EDUCATIONAL SYSTEM

Public education has deteriorated all across our country in the last twenty or thirty years. Much of the failure has to do with the deterioration of our society. There are more broken homes, more children born out of wedlock without a stable two-parent home, and more permissive childrearing with inadequate discipline. Besides this, more couples are working more hours and passing off their children for larger periods of time to nannies, babysitters, and daycare. Once old enough, these children are enrolled in school. It is no wonder that parental influence is at an all-time low. This problem will continue to increase as family life deteriorates and as states expand the number of mandatory hours in school and the number of years for mandatory education. This is a national problem; however, in the city the educational quality is even lower and at the lowest ebb in the inner city.

Where can my children go to school where they will not only get a decent education but where they will be safe as well? If you live in an area where the public education is lacking, it is good to know that there are other options. Most large cities have a number of educational alternatives.

One option is the alternative public schools available in many cities. Magnet and charter schools have become available to students outside the neighborhood boundary restrictions imposed by local public schools. These alternate schools are public schools but usually provide better education than their counterparts. The requirements for admission are stricter, and the requirements to continue one's enrollment are also more demanding; therefore, the gang activity, violence, and drugs are less prevalent. One needs to do a little research to discover the availability and quality of the schools available.

A second alternative is private schools, which are abundant in the city. Some are secular private schools run by private enterprise, but most are religious schools run by various religions, denominations, or churches. These schools also vary in quality but on the average rate higher in the standardized testing than the public schools. These schools have better discipline and usually do not have street gangs, violence, and drug trafficking. Of course, the major drawback is the cost of tuition. Even though the tuition is difficult to manage, many families, with God's help, have found a way. When we came to Chicago, serving as missionaries and living with a low missionary income, which was lower than the average, we were able to enroll both of our children, who were old enough at that time, in a Christian school. Because we worked hard to stay out of debt and lived a frugal life, my wife was able to stay home with our two preschoolers, and we were also able to pay the tuition required. Indeed, God will make a way.

A third alternative is the practice of home education. In the last twenty-five years, homeschooling has skyrocketed in popularity in the United States. With over two million children being homeschooled nationwide, many companies have begun producing quality Christian as well as secular curriculum. Though the restrictions and requirements vary from state to state, the practice of homeschooling is legal in all fifty states and in many countries. Every state also has an organization that provides a state convention for homeschooling with a curriculum exhibit hall as well as information on support groups in the area in which you live. To find out the requirements in the state you live in as well as a number for a state organization representative, contact The Home School Legal Defense Association in Purcellville, Virginia.[1]

One of the great advantages of homeschooling is the enablement it affords parents to protect their children from immoral influences. The Bible says, "Do not be deceived: 'Bad company corrupts good morals'" (1 Cor 15:33; also Ps 1:1–3; Prov 4:14, 13:20). Based on the principles in these passages, it is clear that it is dangerous for parents to allow their children to grow up with massive amounts of time spent with non-believers or even carnal Christians, especially out of the supervision and knowledge of their caring parents. Could this be why so many teens (including Christian teens) are promiscuous, and many young girls become pregnant before completing high school? Could this be why the dropout rate is so high? Could this be why drug and alcohol use is rampant among teens? Homeschooling not only allows parents to have supervision over the education of their children but allows for the guidance of friendships as well.

Even though I am an advocate of homeschooling, I do not believe homeschooling is for everyone. First of all, because of debt it is not possible for some families to have one spouse stay home to educate their children. Secondly, it is necessary that you have good control of your children. Parents with unruly and disobedient children will have a very difficult time trying to supervise their education each day and

1. Home School Assoc.

would find homeschooling to be exasperating. Third, the husband and wife must both be committed to home education. Homeschooling one's children is not easy and takes a major commitment of time and energy. Homeschooling requires perseverance, and for a person to tackle such a great task without the support and blessing, if not the help, of his or her spouse would be very difficult and discouraging.

If you are not comfortable with the public education provided in the area where you live, these three viable alternatives are worthy of serious consideration, especially when moving into the urban environment.

Much of the information in this chapter is from a man's perspective so I asked my wife Debbie if she would summarize some thoughts based on her experiences raising four children in the inner city of Chicago.

A MOTHER'S THOUGHTS ON RAISING CHILDREN IN THE CITY

Having now lived in the inner city of Chicago for the last twenty-nine years, I can say I never wanted to be anywhere else.

As a wife with four children, two sons and two daughters, coming to work here in ministry and being new and alone was a calling of God on my life as well as my husband's.

I felt safe . . . even though life in the inner city has many dangers. Safe—what does that mean? For me it means being in the will of God. In the city, or in any place around the world, we adjust and surrender to the place God sends us.

Even though the city has many parks that provide a place for kids to play, God graciously blessed us with a home that included a nice-sized yard. Our yard became a focal point for the neighborhood children, which offered us opportunities for Christian witness and at the same time allowed us direct supervision of our children.

The primary relationships that our children and teens had came from the church and other families that shared our faith and values. Our children or teens were never alone as they moved around the city; they were either with parents or in a group of trusted peers.

Morality is an issue in every Christian home, but in the city young people are faced with moral issues *very* early. In our house, we spoke openly and early of God's instruction regarding what was right and decent. Nothing was off limits. Our children saw the wickedness of the streets, and our openness was essential in countering these forces of wickedness.

As we raised our children, we allowed urban experiences to be a part of their lives as we involved ourselves in the lives of those around us. Discipling children includes age-appropriate experiences creating many illustrations of how God wants us to minister to the unsaved of this world and to those of the city in particular. Our children accompanied us as we visited the poor, those on drugs or alcohol, troubled families, the sick, and they observed us treating the homeless and prostitutes with respect, even as we invited them, on occasion, for a meal.

The educational choice of homeschooling proved to be a most valuable discipleship tool. This form of education made it possible for interaction with each of our children as God wonderfully used it to develop consistent Christian character. Those hours of discussion on inexhaustible subjects along with many good experiences developed strong Christian character.

Waiting on God's ultimate earthly partner (their spouses) was talked about from early childhood. Believing God had mates specially prepared for them and would bring them into their lives in his timing helped to protect them from the draw of ungodly friendships.

As with all Christian parents our trust in our children was occasionally challenged as their rebellious natures and their sinfulness exerted influence. As Christian parents, we continually confronted sin as we sought God and as he proved to be faithful in putting us in the right place at the right time in order to influence or discipline our children for the decisions they made. Realizing our children's safety and development were wrapped up in God's plan for them allowed us to live with freedom from fear knowing they were God's *before* they were ours.

The love we had for our children was never expressed through permissiveness but rather the qualities expressed in 1 Corinthians 13:4–7. We worked at showing love to each child individually, and at the same time understanding their differences, similarities, and understanding and developing their uniqueness.

As we were faithful to God, we were blessed with these wonderful adult children:

Four virgins . . . who waited on the Lord for their life partners (the youngest, twenty-six-years old, is still looking forward to God's choice for her).

Our oldest daughter is married to our much-loved Puerto Rican son-in-law. They are leaders in an inner city church not far away. So far they have blessed us with seven Grandchildren, ages fifteen and younger.

Our oldest son married our cherished Filipino daughter-in-law. He is an ordained pastor serving in an African American community and one of the worst neighborhoods of our city—much different from the professional basketball player he once dreamed of and prepared to become. They have blessed us with three Grandchildren thus far.

Our second son, the third oldest of our children, serves with his wife, our treasured daughter-in-law, as full time missionaries, directing the children's ministry and serving as administrator at the young church his brother pastors. They have given us two wonderful Grandchildren.

Our second daughter, and youngest, is very involved as a youth worker at our church and a senior educator with a Christian organization teaching abstinence in the public schools of Chicago.

The city has never hurt our children. In fact, God has used it as a potter's stylus, molding them into committed followers of Jesus Christ. "To God be the glory . . . great things he has done."[2]

THE COMMON URBAN PROBLEM OF BURNOUT

The comment "I would rather burn out than rust out" may sound spiritual but the fact is that God does not want us to do either. One of the common plights of urban ministry is the large number of missionary and church staff who experience burnout. Burnout is common among "people-helping" vocations because of emotional and physical demands that are made over long periods of time. Burnout is even more common in urban ministry because the problems and needs people face are more severe, more varied, and more common. The urban minister finds himself making statements like: "There are just too many people to care for." "It's just too much." "We can't seem to make headway." "The problems are too great, and there aren't enough of us to help them."

Some have confused stress with burnout, so we would do well to consider the difference so as to correctly identify both.[3]

2. Sims, *Baptist Hymnal*, 272.

3. Hart, *Clergy Burnout*.

Stress vs. Burnout	
Stress	Burnout
Characterized by overengagement	Characterized by disengagement
Emotions are overreactive	Emotions are blunted
Produces urgency and hyperactivity	Produces helplessness and hopelessness
Loss of energy	Loss of motivation, ideals, and hope
Leads to anxiety disorders	Leads to detachment and depression
Primary damage is physical	Primary damage is emotional
May kill you prematurely	May make life seem not worth living

Many have wondered if they are on the road to burnout. Some may have the symptoms listed above but would like a little more confirmation. **Dr. Archibald D. Hart,** Clinical Psychologist and Senior Professor of Psychology and Dean Emeritus of the Graduate School of Psychology, Fuller Theological Seminary in Pasadena, California, has provided a simple test that can help you determine if your emotions are near burnout. I have provided a copy of this test in Appendix 1 for your use.

What are some things we can do to prevent and cure burnout?

Find rest and encouragement through prayer. There is something about casting your burden on the Lord. In Matthew 11:28–30, Jesus said, "Come to me, all who are weary and heavy-laden, and I will give you rest. Take my yoke upon you and learn from me, for I am gentle and humble in heart, and you will find rest for your souls. For my yoke is easy and my burden is light." Just the act alone of crying out to God relieves much of the burden of ministry let alone the impact as God answers, strengthening and encouraging us.

Find a prayer partner whom you can trust, has an understanding of ministry, and who has a high level of spiritual maturity. This is not only someone you can share your burden with but one who will encourage and pray with and for you. In Galatians 6:2, Paul says, "Bear one another's burdens, and thereby fulfill the law of Christ." Mature brothers are a gift from God that he has provided to help us cope with dangers like burnout.

Take time off. Though he didn't need it, God took a day off for rest as an example to us. Try to get away from home so you will not have interruptions. Make arrangements for others to cover for you so you can really put work behind you. In order to provide for rest, my church not only provides from three to six weeks of vacation for pastors but also an annual Work Week. We use the Work Week to get away and plan, read, and do other work-related (non-people oriented) things. Though this is not a vacation, it is relaxing to be away from the demands of work, counseling, and the telephone. In the fall we participate in what we call the Staff Oasis. This is three full days and nights at a camp for rest and fellowship. No work or meetings are allowed. The purpose is to build staff relationships and provide a restful environment. You may find it difficult to separate yourself from your ministry for these rest and renewal opportunities but it is absolutely necessary. During a time of pressure and intense need, Jesus provided rest and seclusion for his disciples, thereby setting an example for us. He told them, "'Come away by yourselves to a secluded place and rest a while.' (For there were many people coming and going, and they did not even have time to eat.) They went away in the boat to a secluded place by themselves" (Mark 6: 31–32).

It is important to get proper exercise. Exercise alleviates the psychological effects of emotional exhaustion by increasing endorphins that are the brain's natural tranquilizers. Whether you go to the health club, play racquetball, jog, or take a brisk walk, exercise is important in maintaining not only our physical health but our psychological and emotional health as well. Our senior pastor jogs three times a week. I have walked briskly to and from work about five times a week for the past eleven years. This is a total of four miles each day. I couple this walk with prayer making it an excellent time of preparation for my day.

Along with exercise, make sure you get adequate sleep. Contrary to what has been taught in the past, most people need more sleep than what they get. Go to bed at a regular time each evening. Sleep heals the body and has an amazing ability to renew you physically, mentally, and emotionally.

Learn to prioritize your time. This means that sometimes we must say *no*. I had to learn that everything is not urgent. I have found that the really important things, things that will impact eternity, are seldom urgent. We allow the emergencies to crowd out those important things in life. Sometimes other staff or even lay people can assist in some of the needs. Often when we postpone caring for something that is not really urgent, it is resolved without our assistance. Don't feel you always have to answer the phone. That's why we have voice mail and e-mail. What would be a thirty-minute phone conversation may only need a quick response by leaving a voice message or by sending a response by texting. Keep a To-Do List to help you complete the needed tasks and finally, arrange for your prayer and study time to be protected from interruptions.

Take time out for yourself, your wife, and children. Having a date night with your wife and a family night with the kids where you plan something fun breaks the monotony and helps you forget about the burdens. Participation in recreational activities or hobbies will also help you to release these psychological and emotional burdens of ministry.

Last but not least, it is vital that we maintain a regular time with God. Your quiet time feeds your spirit. It renews you from within and gives God a means to speak to you. That said, you need more than a quick devotional. Start each day with a personal Bible study and prayer time. There are many methods but choose one that works for you. I like to journal my way through the Bible, writing down what the passage is saying, the implications, and what I should do in response. This method helps me focus, stay awake, and benefit from my study time. I like to use my laptop computer so I can save my journal and, when desired, use my computer Bible study program with the many study resources. I often look up word meanings, read commentary analysis, and use my computerized concordance. In short, maintaining a close relationship with Christ is by far the most important thing we can do to prevent burnout. Your quiet time will help you to maintain a sense of priority and purpose in all that you do.

REVIEW QUESTIONS

1. What aspect of the theology of God is applicable to those who move to an urban area?
2. List three wise practices from the chapter that you would implement if you were going to raise a family in the city.
3. According to the author, where should one live when serving the Lord in the city?
4. Why is burnout more common in urban ministry?
5. What do you believe to be the three greatest practices that would most prevent burnout?

11

Planting an Urban Church, Part 1

God's Institutional Design for Reaching Beyond

God's plan for implementing the Great Commission is through the local church. There is no plan B. When the Apostle Paul traveled the Roman Empire, his objective was to plant local churches. The people in these churches were to carry out the Great Commission. There were no mission boards or church planting agencies. The churches themselves sent men out to plant churches. In the book of Acts, Paul and Barnabas were exposed to the urban church at Antioch for a year (Acts 11:26) before the church, directed by the Holy Spirit, sent them out on the First Missionary Journey (Acts 13:2–3). The church at Antioch, as the sending church, was where Paul returned after each missionary journey. It was his base of operation before he left on successive trips (the Second Missionary Journey, Acts 15:35–36 and the Third Missionary Journey, Acts 18:22–23). This is not an exposé against para-church organizations. I believe God uses these organizations, and because of the lack of resources and the way most churches are set up, there is a need for these agencies. Most churches have relegated their responsibility for others to cover, which heightens the need for this vacuum to be filled.

In biblical times, the elderly parents were taken care of by their children. In modern times when nursing homes sprang up, children that should have taken care of that responsibility found it easier to pay an organization to be surrogate custodians, taking care of the responsibilities God intended for them to have (1 Tim 5:3–8). At one time it was the responsibilities of the church and its members to help needy people. Adult children felt the responsibility to take care of their elderly parents. In fact even until the mid twenty-first century, only the rich could afford to place their loved ones in private respectable homes. Middle class and poor people had to send their parents to state institutions called "alms-houses" or "poor farms." I say "respectable homes" because almshouses had a stigma attached to them because of the dilapidated facilities and poor care they provided. When the Social Security Act was signed in 1935 some subsidy was provided. Later, with the creation of Medicare in 1969 followed by subsequent legislation, Medicare became the financial source making it possible for most elderly adults to be placed into these residential centers.[1] Therefore, when the government and non-profit organizations began stepping in to meet this need, the church and the children of the elderly conveniently bowed out (Deut 14:28–29; Acts 6:1–7; 1 Tim 6:17–19; 1 John 3:17). When churches abrogated the responsibility to take care of parentless children, orphanages sprang up. In James 1:27, in the context of being doers of the Word (Jas 1:22–25), the writer assumes that once you visit the orphan or widow who are in distress, you do more than encourage and pray; you seek to help them with the problem or need.

When someone steps up to do the job, it is human nature to step aside and let them do it. Often these organizations spring up because the church has not met the needs they were supposed to meet. Today, despite the plethora of organizations planting churches, they do not eliminate our responsibility. This is especially true in the American urban setting because few organizations are doing an adequate and successful job of planting churches. How much more effective for a church that has been successful in this environment to replicate its ministry, providing the team support and knowledge to operate a successful ministry. The church is "God's Institutional Design for Reaching Beyond" our borders to people outside our area. We should not only multiply people but also multiply our ministry.

For years we have watched men move into the large urban setting to plant churches. We have estimated that 90 percent of these well-meaning missionaries were unsuccessful. After a few years they gave up or burned out, leaving their mission with a few poor souls hurt and wondering: What happened to our mentors? Why did they fail? Why did they burn out, hurting their ministries and us?

First, the urban church planter usually does not come with team support. To move into a larger city brings a host of unexpected problems

1. Nursing Homes, PBS, 1–2.

like loneliness, fear, cultural shock, and burnout. Because there is no team, there is no support system. The missionary and his wife feel alone and have difficulty with the isolation and discouragement.

Second, the church planter has inadequate training. He may have had a class or classes on urban ministry in college or seminary but few schools provide the hands-on training needed to be successful in a larger urban environment. If he has some experience, it was in a small city and often had no supervision and guidance from experienced urban ministers. No one explained to him how to deal with the hostile urban culture and how to face problems with urban living conditions. No course in school can properly prepare you to live in this environment. That's why our church started the C.A.U.S.E. program (Chicago Armitage Urban Study Experience) more than twenty years ago. In this program we offer a three-month and a one-year internship program that will immerse the student in urban living.

Third, most urban missionaries are not prepared for the intimidating urban living conditions; conditions like finding decent affordable housing, and finding a school where you feel your children will not only get a good education but where they will be safe. They did not expect to find an environment where they would be concerned about the safety of their children outside of the home.

Fourth, if the missionary was living on financial support, the supporting agencies sometimes gave the missionary a deadline that was too short to become self-supporting. One agency gives the missionary support for two years. This is woefully inadequate for most large urban church planters, especially if he is in a poor area. After the two years are over the missionary has to seek employment or leave the field completely.

Finally, the missionary often doesn't come with a long-term mindset. They think it will be a cakewalk planting a church where there are masses of people all around. They don't come with the determination to stick it out and to find a way to make it in the urban environment.

WHAT TYPE OF A CHURCH SHOULD I BEGIN?

Should I begin a traditional church or follow the cell or house church model? There are numerous books written to promote the home church model. It is not my intention to elaborate on this model but I would encourage the reader to study good books on this topic. Though the house location provides an excellent way to begin an urban church, I find that they quickly exceed their home capacity, and it becomes difficult to train leaders quickly enough to fill the need for church leaders so that the church can expand into new assemblies. Perhaps in an urban setting the best approach is to begin in the home but, as the space fills up, rent or purchase a small building near the original starting location.

Because the city is culturally diverse how can I reach people from different ethnic groups? Non-Caucasian ethnics compose over half the population of the United States. These include Hispanics, African Americans, Native Americans, Japanese, Chinese, Filipinos, Indian, Jewish, and many other groups. The heaviest concentration of these ethnic groups resides in urban areas. If you are going to plant a church in the city, you will undoubtedly have to plant a church that will attract people of minority ethnic descent. These groups do not easily assimilate into the culture of a Caucasian church. How can we develop a ministry that will most effectively reach people of different ethnic groups? First, let us discuss seven different models for reaching urban ethnics. These models, except for number five and seven, come from the article written by Tetsunao Yamamori titled *How to Reach Urban Ethnics.*[2]

1. The Assimilationist Model

This is by far the most common approach used in American churches today. Many churches say that they are open to people of all ethnic groups to attend their church. But what do they mean? They may welcome visitors but they are basically saying that if they are to continue coming, they must assimilate, to fit in, and "become like us." There will be little attempt to alter the ministry or to adjust to the needs and preferences of other cultures.

2. Yamamori, *Mission*, 29

White, Anglo-Saxon, Protestant (WASP) churches receive members almost entirely from people who have a low intensity of "ethnic consciousness." In other words its members fit in well with the WASP culture and do not see themselves as principally different from it, regardless of their race. Those in an ethnic group who are social-economically upward in mobility tend to associate themselves with the Anglo churches and are comfortable in them.

For example, African Americans who approximate WASP standards are racially African American but are culturally white, and are often happy in Anglo churches. Assimilationist churches attract a few people but repel many others. If this is the most common approach in America, is there any wonder why we are not reaching ethnic people in the larger cities of our country?

2. Mono-ethnic House Churches

In this model, the Anglo church extends its ministry by developing house churches, Bible study groups, and prayer cells among the ethnic neighborhoods. In time, several house churches may group together to start their own church. They may hold services in the parenting Anglo church or may rent or purchase a separate building. This is a homogeneous, ethnic approach to church planting.

3. Autonomous Mono-ethnic Church within an Anglo Church

In this model, an Anglo church starts an ethnic service within its own building developing into a mono-ethnic Church. As they grow, they usually move out into their own facility.

Uptown Baptist Church on Chicago's northeast side is an example of this kind of church. For a number of years they have operated churches ministering to various people groups. Currently these ethnic groups include English-speaking, Spanish-speaking, Vietnamese, Russian, and African congregations.

4. Ethnically Changing Churches—Transitional Community

The neighborhood in which I have lived for the past twenty-six years, located in the inner city of Chicago, has been in transition for over one hundred years. At one time it was a Jewish community that transitioned into a Swedish neighborhood. The Swedish-speaking people learned English, which eventually changed the language of the community. Then the composition of the community changed again from Swedish to Hispanic. The people moving in were Puerto Rican, many being second and third generation, which means that most spoke English. Then the transition began to change again to African American.

Now, with major urban renewal taking place in my neighborhood, it is changing to more of an Anglo community with young professionals buying vacant lots and building two-story, single family homes and condos. This kind of transition is common in large cities.

The Anglo church in a community where there is a high ethnic inflow will soon notice a changing composition in its neighborhood. There is a major decrease of people from the original Anglo culture because many of their members moved to the suburbs. As the transition continues, the neighborhood becomes more like the new ethnic group that is moving in. The attendance in the original church has taken a major hit and there may be a few from the new culture that has assimilated in. The church has experienced a gaping hole. Often there is a sense of resentment and loss as the church continues to decline. This transitional experience can be multiplied hundreds of times all across the United States. Ethnically changing community churches often experience spiritual, psychological, and financial difficulties due to decreasing membership, reduced budgets, broken friendships, and fear.

Faced with the changing of the community, the transitional church must make one of four choices. One option is to disband the church and to simply close down. This may be a viable, if not desirable option, and if change isn't done quickly they will likely be forced into this decision.

A second option is for the church to relocate to another site, probably out of the transitional area. If the church decides to do this it would be important, for the sake of the new ethnic group, to plant a new ethnic church in the old location reaching the people they would be unable to impact.

Third, some churches in ethnically changing communities have merged with other churches in the area to pool resources. This can probably solve some immediate problems but is not a good solution from a church growth perspective. The past problems of both churches will continue with the new merger. Depending on the size of the ethnic expansion, this solution may not be long-term as the Anglo church continues to decline. I have known a number of churches that have done this type of merger successfully, but only in neighborhoods where ethnic expansion had greatly slowed down. Even though they were successful, each merger came with much difficulty. For a church considering this option it is important that both merging congregations are committed to serve local residents and support the church for the existence of this ministry. Also, in many cases the merger will not be a permanent fix. As the community continues to change, the need will be for the church to learn to reach out and minister to the new residents in the neighborhood.

A final solution for churches in ethnically changing communities is to stay in the community and try to adapt. This will be very difficult if the incoming ethnic group does not speak English. If a good percentage of the new ethnic group speaks English, I believe this option is one that deserves serious consideration. To adapt to the changing environment, the people in the existing church must be committed to serve the local residents. This means visually incorporating people from the new ethnic group into your ministry and, as soon as possible, into your leadership. It must become public knowledge that your church is committed to adapt to a new kind of ministry that is friendly to the new ethnic culture. There must not be any prejudicial attitudes and the members who decide to stay with the church must embrace the new group with a commitment to reach, love, and serve them.

5. Multisite Ethnic Congregations Inhabiting a Single Church Building or at Various Sites

Each ethnic church contributes to the "umbrella church" in finance, ministry, and government; and each church has its own congregation, pastor, and lay leaders. Often the branches of the umbrella church will periodically worship together and engage in common ministries. At Armitage, even though we are a multicultural church, we have been conducting both the Sunday worship and adult Bible studies in the Spanish language for over twelve years. These services are all held in our building. Adult children of Spanish speaking parents in America often prefer English so, even though their parents are in the Spanish services, the children attend the English service and Bible studies. This is true of other ethnic groups as well and this type of arrangement can provide a healthy cooperative relationship. We are also developing multisite congregations in remote locations around the city.

6. Single/Multiple Sponsorship Mono-ethnic Churches

This model represents a local ethnic church that is sponsored and supported in its early stage by a single church or group of churches.

One or more mother churches

Mono-ethnic daughter churches

7. Multicultural Church

In this model, the church incorporates, not assimilates, multiple ethnic groups as part of its ministry. The church embraces the different ethnicity and seeks to serve and reach whoever God has placed in their community. It is not "them and us," it is The Body of Christ. Multi-ethnicity is our culture in the American cities and is becoming our culture in the suburbs and small towns, as well. We cannot continue to develop our churches as segregated monoculture, ethnocentric entities. If our Wal-Mart is multicultural, our churches can be multicultural, as well. It is time the church in the United States begins to reach each people group, and I believe one of the most effective approaches is through multicultural churches.

When Charles Lyons came to Armitage Baptist Church thirty-five years ago, the church was composed of twenty-five Appalachian, white congregants. At the time of this writing we host nearly one thousand people every Sunday morning, most worshipping together in English. Armitage is a true multicultural church with thirty-seven different nationalities on a given Sunday morning. Currently, 40 percent of our people make up numerous Caucasian nationalities, 38 percent are various Hispanic groups, 15 percent African American, 4 percent Asian, and 3 percent make up various other groups. Pastor Lyons had no books or seminars to instruct him how to develop a multicultural church. He learned as the church grew, seeking to reach whoever lived in our multicultural part of the city.

In this model, we learn to understand, appreciate, and enjoy God's creative genius. As I explained in chapter 4 on "Principles of Urban Ministry," Principle Four says that God has a love for every ethnic group on the face of the earth. He created each one and sent his son to die for the people of each group. As I stated in that chapter, the model of the early church at Antioch was a multicultural model, and I believe we need to make strides to develop this model wherever possible.

What should be done when the new ethnic group does not speak the language of the existing church? There are several approaches that churches have taken in order to reach people when there is a language barrier. One is to translate the message. The preacher speaks in one language and pauses while it is translated. Though some have followed this procedure, it is difficult to use this method. First of all, translating a sermon doubles the length of time of the sermon. Second, it is simply too hard for the people to benefit from the message when it is constantly interrupted with another translation. Most of the existing people will become disgruntled and find another church, and at the same time the new ethnic group will be slow to embrace messages presented in this way.

Some churches have provided silent translation by way of a wireless earpiece. In this method the church stations a translator with earphones in a soundproof booth listening to the message and translating into a microphone. The non-English speaking participant listens through an earpiece as the message is being translated into his language. We have used this method in our Sunday evening services and have not found it to be widely embraced. The ethnic person does not like hearing an alien language in one ear with a delayed translation in the other ear.

The main approach we have used is to provide a special service in the language of the non-English speaking person. For example, we have recruited a bilingual man fluent in English and Spanish who is the pastor of the Spanish speaking congregation. Since most of the children prefer English, they attend the English Bible studies and service with their English speaking friends. This segregated approach, though not multicultural, is the only method we have found to be successful in reaching people who do not speak the language of the existing church. This approach provides for the needs of the non-English speaking people and at the same time provides for the needs of other family members who prefer the English services.

What are some of the necessary changes we need to make if we are going to plant or transition our church to be multicultural? First, to transition an existing congregation to become a multicultural church we need to go through a period of training. The existing people should know the biblical basis of a multicultural church, its necessity, what to expect, and how to react as people of the new ethnic group begin to attend our church. We need to help our people learn to respect the new culture, seek to be "incarnational," to learn to love these new people as our brothers and sisters in Christ, and to be willing to release control and evolve into a church that is "new culture friendly." The church desiring to be a multicultural church needs to focus on evangelizing and discipling people, not Americanizing them.

Second, it helps to begin inviting preachers from the ethnic group you are attempting to reach, filling the pulpit in the language of the existing church, which in this country is English. This will help the people become more accepting and build respect for the new culture.

Third, revise any printed material, making it clear that your new neighbors, who are part of the new ethnic group, are welcome. If pictures are included, make sure that members of the ethnic group are included—fellowshipping or serving—with some of the existing church members. The goal is to depict harmony and acceptance. The picture should not give the impression of the ethnic person as a token member of his race but that he is truly part of the church.

Fourth, recruit people from the new ethnic group to serve in visible positions as soon as possible. Even though they might not be spiritually mature they might be suited to serve as a greeter or usher. As God provides, recruit ethnic people with a consistent Christian life to serve on the platform reading scripture, giving announcements, playing instruments, and leading the worship service. As they become available, the new ethnic group should provide godly teachers, deacons, and other elected church officers as well as part-time and eventually full-time staff members from that ethnic group, as well. By involving people in visible positions it assures the new ethnic group that they are truly welcomed, their culture is respected, and it is becoming their church. It should be the goal to have the workers, including the leadership, reflect the racial composition of your church. I am not talking about a system of quotas; the goal is to find qualified people who are called by God.

Fifth, it is important to build the needed ethnic influence into the worship of the church. Every church seeking to be multicultural needs to find its predominant style, or core style of, music. Along with the core music, a multicultural church may have a variety of specific types of music that various ethnic groups in attendance enjoy. Additional styles or selections may be added to the core. Hymns are predominately a Western/Anglo form of worship. We have not totally eliminated them, but we have found that contemporary worship is more effective in our multicultural service. We often even give the old hymns a contemporary flare. We do not accept the premise that contemporary music is evil. We believe music to be neutral; the words, however, must be doctrinally and biblically accurate.

With our contemporary core, we often include various entrées of ethnic music. For example, because of the large number of Hispanics in our services, we use guitars, tambourines, congas, and kettledrums as well as brass instruments. We sometimes sing songs in Spanish to affirm the Spanish heritage. Because of the African American people in our congregation, we sing gospel songs. We even have several songs in the Swahili language, which comes from the country of Kenya, affirming those with African heritage. Because we have chosen a participatory form of worship, we use very little special music. Once a year we have what we call our All Church Sing after our evening service where we feature many volunteer performers. Recently, at this event we had a Mexican choir dressed in traditional outfits singing a Mexican song in Spanish and English, a solo of one of our African American ladies singing a gospel song, a man playing a classical song on his banjo, and a young man performing a Christian rap that he wrote himself. As you can see, a multicultural church seeks to include every group to its worship and ministry.

Sixth, our preaching ministry includes a balance between teaching and inspiration. Without being stereotypical, I think it is true that Caucasian and Asian people tend to look for teaching in the sermons. They like to leave the service thinking they learned something, while African American and Hispanic ethnic groups tend to look more for inspiration. If a typical white person were to visit an African American church, the participation, response, and emotionalism may be too much for them to feel comfortable. On the other hand, if an African American person visited a typical white church, he would become bored because of the lack of participation and inspiration, along with the heavy theological instruction from many expository sermons that often accompany those services. Depending on the composition, many multicultural services need to combine both elements of teaching and inspiration.

Our senior pastor Charles Lyons is very good at combining both elements in our services. His messages are both educational as well as inspirational. It is also important that the messages, as well as the entire service, affirm the culture of the people present. In doing this, our pastor is careful that he does not use illustrations that could be misunderstood. For example, he suggests that an illustration about cowboys and Indians may cause our Native American brothers and sisters in our congregation to wonder who the good guy is. His illustrations often reflect the ethnic people he is addressing, making sure that the good guy is not always the white man. He stays away from stereotypes because they are not accurate and are often degrading. Because he is speaking to urban people he uses urban expressions like "high-rise building," "condo," "second story flat," or "the projects" instead of suburban jargon like "split-level or "tri-level," or "cul-de-sac." That is why it is so important to be "incarnational" as we talked about in chapter 3 on "Principles of Urban Ministries." When we are "incarnational," we really understand the people, and we speak the way they speak because we are one with them. Finally, when preaching, make sure that your vocabulary is understood by the new ethnic group. Avoid explanations that are difficult to understand from the Greek and Hebrew grammar. This is not the time to show off your vast vocabulary or intellect. Just preach the Word of God in a very practical and understandable way so your congregation can grasp it and put it into practice in their lives.

Seventh, pray that the Holy Spirit will empower your church to realize the lostness of every person without Christ and to act intentionally to encourage ethnic church growth.

As is evident, there are many types of urban church structures. Once your philosophy and structure is agreed upon, it is time to begin the hard work of selecting a team and beginning a healthy growing church, as we will discuss in the next chapter.

REVIEW QUESTIONS

1. What are five reasons the author gives to explain why most urban church plants fail?
2. What is the major problem of growing a church using the house church model?
3. Though most common, why is the Assimilationist Model the least effective in reaching people of different ethnic groups?
4. Why should a church consider becoming a multicultural church?
5. What are some of the changes we need to make if we are going to plant or transition our church to be multicultural?

12

Planting an Urban Church, Part 2

Hitting the Road Running

Now that we are in agreement as to the philosophical approach and structure to follow in planting an urban church, it's time to begin recruiting team members, both full-time staff members and lay volunteers.

SELECTING A TEAM

When should we begin selecting a team to reach people in an urban setting? By team members, I am referring to people who will accept the position as full-time staff members of the new church. Simply stated, church leaders should recruit team members when they have people who are spiritually equipped and ready. When the timing is right God will raise up leaders. Far too often church leaders run ahead of God and force a church to start ahead of God's timetable causing damage and failure. In 1Timothy 5:22, the Apostle Paul warned the young pastor of the danger of appointing immature, unqualified, and unprepared leaders when he said, "Do not lay hands upon anyone too hastily and thereby share responsibility for the sins of others."

Second, church leaders are ready to select a team when they have general direction and a basic philosophy. Will they plant a house church and continue this approach by dividing to form a new house church when they are at capacity? Will they grow the church into a more traditional church, eventually meeting in a building holding traditional services? If the new location is in an ethnically diverse area, which of the seven church models listed in the preceding chapter will they be planting? Will church leaders follow the traditional church planting approach of sending a team out to plant a separate indigenous church or will they follow a multisite church model? How will the church expenses and staff salaries be funded? Some larger churches provide salaries until the church is able to carry that expense but many urban church planters raise missionary support through missionary agencies or by independent effort. These and other questions need to be answered before one has gone very far into the process of planting a new church.

Finally, it is almost too obvious to state, but let it be said that any attempt to select team members should be preceded with much prayer. Before Christ selected his twelve disciples, he spent the entire night in prayer (Luke 6:12–13). How much more do we need divine guidance?

What training is necessary for those serving as staff members of an urban team? Not only should the team members be spiritually mature, but we also need to select men who are qualified educationally. The lead person who will be the senior pastor should have the academic training in biblical studies, theology, and ministry. I'm also convinced that the urban church planter needs to have a strong internship to equip him to be successful in this hostile environment. The academic training provided by most Bible colleges and seminaries is not enough. Field training is necessary for foreign missionaries. Likewise, the need is just as great in this foreign mission field of the city.

Internship should be more than a few weeks or months, especially if the person has not lived for an extended period of time in a large city. An internship where the person lives and serves in the city for an entire year will prepare him for a successful and fruitful ministry. The content of his training should include a variety of urban books and tapes, field trips to various successful urban ministries, interviews with experienced staff, seminars provided by staff on various aspects of urban ministry, and shadowing staff, especially in one's chosen specialty. Shadowing affords the intern the opportunity to be in close proximity to see what the pastor does and how he responds in many situations. For an internship to be most effective there should be an experienced pastor or staff person to mentor the intern into that ministry. Finally, a good internship will afford the person an opportunity to serve in a capacity that will involve him in the ministry emphasis he believes he is called to. This should include critical evaluation providing correction and encouragement.

Academic qualifications of non-pastoral team members are also very helpful but are important to a lesser degree. Some team members may emerge from the mother church, and have been raised and trained in the urban environment. Once they become spiritually mature they may become part of an effective team.

Whom should we select to be on the church planting team? Always look for people with a proven reputation for godliness and integrity, and people who are filled with the Holy Spirit. It is difficult to discover this simply by studying an application, reading referral letters, or by a personal interview. It is much better to observe the candidate for a time. It is ideal to recruit people from your own church because you have already observed them. At Armitage, we do this through our internship program. If the only option is the interview process, do your homework, talking to referrals, past employers, and academic supervisors.

Second, they must meet the biblical requirements found in 1 Timothy 3:1–7 and Titus 1:6–9. Obviously, the standard is higher for people who will fill major positions, especially as church leadership staff. Lay people should be discipled to grow into these standards but, depending on the responsibility, may not be held to the same requirements. If these requirements are given serious consideration, many ministry problems and destructive experiences can be avoided.

Third, they must be in agreement doctrinally and philosophically. Many ministers have come on staff with a church or missionary agency only to find out that they were not compatible. Ask the hard questions and listen to the advice and opinions of other people.

Fourth, look for people who are already doing ministry. They have proven their commitment to ministry by their actions. These people may not have served in a vocational ministry position but are committed to, and experienced in, serving the Lord in a church setting.

Fifth, look for faithful men and women—faithful to the Lord and faithful to the task they have committed to complete. Paul said, "The things which you have heard from me in the presence of many witnesses, entrust these to faithful men who will be able to teach others also" (2 Tim 2:2).

Sixth, they must be willing to move into the neighborhood and live among the people you are seeking to reach. It is not effective to commute from a plush neighborhood to a poor community in the inner city.

Seventh, they must have a determination to stick with it. Longevity is especially important for the full-time leadership. Because growing a church and discipling people takes time, they must plan on sticking with it, persevering through the hard times.

HOW SHOULD I BEGIN TO PLANT A CHURCH?

First, exegete your target community so you will understand its characteristics and needs. This includes demographics (racial/ethnic breakdown, age, socio-economic makeup), history, and needs. With the availability of the Internet, much preliminary information is readily available. Talking to some of the longtime residents can also provide valuable information and at the same time provide an opportunity to establish rapport. Ask them to list the biggest problems and the greatest needs in the community.

Second, as mentioned above, have each full-time leadership staff member move into the target area where the church will be planted. This is necessary in order to meet the needs associated with being incarnational as discussed in chapter 3, titled "Principles of Urban Ministry."

Third, begin getting acquainted with the people in the community. Walk the community. Introduce yourself to people in their yards and on their porches. Prayer walk through your community on a regular basis. This could be done individually or with full-time and volunteer staff, grouped by two or three so as not to obstruct the sidewalk.

Fourth, become servants to the residents. Plan servant outreaches in the community. We have brought in groups from churches in other states to pick up trash, clean the park, and by permission only, clean neighborhood yards. One of our church planters recently put on a carnival at a local park, inviting the neighborhood people to come. Many games and activities were planned, along with plenty of food. The afternoon ended with a program and a raffle drawing of numerous prizes. This provided a way to gain the addresses and phone numbers of residents for follow-up visitation, totaling about three hundred contacts. The carnival also provided a great introduction and a great impression of the new church in the minds of the community residents.

Outreach Ideas

Outreach can show genuine concern for the community and build a positive attitude so that the church has credibility as they seek to reach the people. Here are some ideas for effective outreaches:

- Host a "Free Carwash—No Donations Accepted!"
- Feed parking meters, leaving a card that reads, "Your parking meter looked hungry, so I fed it!" Of course, the name, address, and phone number of the church should be included.[1]
- Discount gasoline. Make an arrangement with the gas station owner to lower the gas by a specified amount, perhaps twenty-five cents a gallon, for several hours. In our outreach we simply gave the first two hundred cars a certificate for twenty dollars worth of gas paid for by a private donation. During the outreach we had a crew there to pump gas, wash windshields, and check oil. We gave each person a slip of paper saying, "Compliments of Armitage Church" with the church location and scheduled meeting times. When we organized our discount gasoline outreach, the day began with a long line of cars waiting in line. Our team of volunteers visited each car answering questions, passing out literature, and sharing the gospel where there seemed to be an open opportunity. It was a very successful outreach allowing us to spread good will in our neighborhood and affording many opportunities for a good gospel witness.
- One of our church planters gave away soft drinks with a card that gave the name, address, and phone number of the church. His staff set up a cooler outside a Subway station. They also went to Starbucks and Dunkin' Donuts, giving them a hundred dollars for complimentary coffee until the money was used up. He had people there to greet customers, tell them about our church, and witness when the opportunity lent itself to do so.
- For one outreach we sent teams up and down the street with a three-step program. First, we passed out flyers telling them that the next day we would be by to clean the street, picking up papers. If requested, we would also pick up papers in their front and back yards. The flyer said we would also be available to mow lawns free of charge when requested. The next day we brought out the crew to pick up papers and mow lawns. The third day we blanketed the neighborhood with invitations to our Super Summer Time pro-

1. Sjögren, *Loving*, 132.

gram (like traditional Vacation Bible School), which we held two weeks later for children during the day and teens in the evening.

- We have teamed up with Prison Fellowship and their Angel Tree program along with a suburban church. The objective was to provide a Christmas program for children who have a parent in prison. Angel Tree provided contact information for families in our zip code area. The suburban church provided the Christmas gifts, and we invited the families to a Christmas party we organized. Of course, we saved the information for additional follow-up and ministry to these contacts.
- We have teamed up with suburban churches that have provided Thanksgiving baskets and turkeys that were distributed to needy families in our area. We have found it important to be careful when providing frozen turkeys and boxed, brand new toys to families where one of the parents is a drug addict. Some addicted parents have sold toys or turkeys for drugs. To prevent this misuse we have actually cooked the turkeys for certain families and allowed the children to open and play with the toys in our presence or at the party so they would be less likely to be sold.
- We sometimes get permission to close off the street to host a neighborhood block party. At this party we provide free food, games for children, face painting, balloons, and carnival games. Sometimes we set up a volleyball net in the street and have even rented a dunk tank. If you do this outreach, be sure to station plenty of people there to talk to the onlookers and participants. If you are reaching out to people of another ethnic group, have plenty of people there with the same ethnicity or who speak their language.
- For many good ideas for outreach, see the Servant Evangelism Web site at: www.servantevangelism.com/matrix/matrix.htm.

Continuing our discussion, the fifth step consists of the church planter visiting the people in his target area. This is for the purpose of getting acquainted and inviting them to a Bible study.

Sixth, start a Bible study. It would be profitable to begin a short-term seeker (evangelistic) Bible study for non-believers or a growth Bible study for Christians. As you grow, add more weeknight Bible studies. An evening prayer meeting will also be important for those who are believers.

Seventh, begin discipling baby Christians. God may draw a few spiritually mature people from the area to join your effort, but most of your leaders will have to be homegrown. This can be accomplished through small groups and one-on-one discipleship (see chapter 5, titled "Calibrating Our Compass"). Be persistent and patient, growth takes time. Satan will attempt to discourage you and thwart your work. If you stick to it, God will bless your efforts.

Eighth, when you have forty or fifty attendees, you are ready to launch a Sunday morning service. It is better to hold out until the number of people is as big as possible. A new church that begins with seventy-five people will build much more excitement and motivation than a group of fifteen. You will undoubtedly have to rent a building for this weekly service. Make sure that this opening meeting is well planned with greeters and worship or praise music led by one or more musicians. Contemporary music led with a guitar will be most effective to meet the needs of urban people, especially in a multicultural setting. As you are able, introduction of a praise band will be well received.

Ninth, after you launch your morning services, you may want to begin Bible studies for various age groups. Most of the materials available are not conducive for inner city needs. Because families move more often, they do not have a consistent church to assist in religious instruction. Along with the lack of church assistance, the religious and biblical training is not met at home; therefore, they usually have little biblical understanding. To complicate the problem, many urban children, especially in the inner city, do not have the reading and problem-solving skills that most church curricula assume. Many ministries are forced to choose a curriculum that is under the age level, which may not suit the child's physiological and social development. Another problem with most curricula is that it is written and designed for children who live in suburban and small town environment. The layout graphics and design do not express the culture and ethnic diversity displayed in the cities. Because of the above problems many teachers have been forced to write their own materials.

There are two companies that are producing quality urban materials for African American children of all age groups that address the above problems: Urban Ministries, Inc. in Chicago, and David C. Cook with their line of materials called "Echoes." Along with curriculum, they also provide conferences and training for church leaders and teachers.

SMALL GROUP STRATEGY AS A CHURCH PLANTING TOOL

One church growth model suggests that a church begin many small group Bible studies that should grow to capacity then, in turn, multiply into additional individual groups. Once there are three or four groups in one area, steps can be taken to begin a church. Each group has a leader and an assistant, with the assistant prepared to eventually take a new group. The groups meet from one-and-a-half to two hours and include fellowship, Bible study, and a prayer segment. Each area organizes an occasional outreach with the other groups in the area for the purpose of fellowship and an opportunity to bring neighbors, relatives, and co-workers. This helps to grow a unity between the area groups with the prospect of uniting as a church. Visitors at the outreach can be invited to come to one of the groups. Each area should have a director whose job is to coach the group leaders, helping them improve quality, select curriculum, and solve problems.

Some churches have found success with this model; however, it has also failed in many parts of the country as a church planting strategy.

THE MULTISITE CONGREGATION APPROACH TO CHURCH PLANTING

One of the problems of urban church planting is that the vast majority of efforts across America have failed. Some of the ways to avoid mistakes and failure are listed at the beginning of this chapter. Another solution that some have adopted is a multisite church planting model. The mother church goes to a needed area, often where the church already has a number of their parishioners and, with the leadership of a campus pastor, establishes a new congregation of their church using some of the steps listed above. Each campus is a branch of the multisite church.

This church organizational structure can be supported in the book of Acts. The early church had no buildings but met in homes. The church at Jerusalem was spread out in many homes with hundreds of people, but was essentially one church governed by the apostles and leaders.

This method provides numerous advantages. First, it provides a support system from the other church pastors as well as members of the church, including those who live in the target area. Second, the mother church can provide support such as bookkeeping, chairs, audiovisual equipment, computers, printers, and finances when available. The church or departments in the church may organize projects raising money for projectors, musical instruments, and other needs. Third, denominational contacts and churches may provide short-term missionary teams, financial support, and project fundraising. Fourth, guidance is available from experienced church staff if problems arise. Fifth, there is a local body providing accountability to insure ethical and wise stewardship as well as productive ministry.

For this strategy to be successful it is necessary for the church to rally around the effort and for the leaders of the mother church to make few demands on the time of the campus pastor. This is necessary to allow him to spend the time needed to develop the new ministry.

In some multisite churches the head pastor preaches, with the message available live over the Internet and projected to each multisite congregation. In those churches the campus pastor leads the service before and after the message. In most churches the campus pastor also recruits a live worship team that leads worship for that particular site. In other multisite churches each campus pastor preaches the same message with appropriate application, while still in other congregations the campus pastor may each preach separate sermons.

The multisite church planting strategy is being used successfully by many urban churches throughout the United States and should be considered a viable method for producing effective urban churches.

THE GREATEST HINDRANCE TO EFFECTIVE CHURCH PLANTING IN THE CITIES

I believe the greatest hindrance to effective church planting in the cities is the culturally inbred desire for the American Dream, which keep men and women from coming to an undesirable and less comfortable environment. For thirty-seven years I have watched many people choose to go to places of comfort rather than places of greatest need. I have watched a large disproportional number of men seeking to go to warm climates rather than less appealing parts of the country. We have struggled to find people willing to consider moving to urban areas where half of the population resides; instead, they choose in favor of less populated parts of the country. Why are so few willing to invest their lives in urban areas? Why are so many shunning the inner cities of our world? Some people require places that can provide a safe environment. Others desire a destination that provides better education for their children. Some hate the thought of the traffic, congestion, smaller yards, and tighter living. Others embrace the common thinking that the city would not be a good environment to raise their children. I have watched some men choose a higher salary and lower cost of living, neither being characteristic of urban ministry. The Lord is searching for the disciples of Christ who are willing to heed the words of Jesus when he said, "If anyone wishes to come after Me, he must deny himself, and take up his cross daily and follow Me" (Luke 9:23). Large cities in every country are grossly understaffed with missionaries and church planters. I believe many have lied to themselves, taking God's second or third choice, believing they have yielded to God's calling. If half of the population of the world is in the cities, the greatest need is to reach these people. Where will an adequate number of future missionaries and pastors come from if we avoid these great population centers?

Once our urban missionaries arrive, they often try to insulate themselves from the harsh urban environment. On the foreign mission field they often live in gated missionary compounds with locals serving as servants and housekeepers. Is this what we referred to as being "incarnational"? We do the same thing in the United States. Some live in the suburbs and commute. Those who serve in ministries, requiring that they live in the city, choose communities that are the nicest possible, moving as far away from the inner city as they can. This attitude brings the impression to the residents that the missionary or pastor has a sense of superiority, breaking down communication, trust, and the potential for a relationship. It prevents the bonding and respect needed to be effective in the urban environment. This is especially true if one is called to reach the inner cities in America and other cities of the world where most of the people are poor. Holding on to our affluence and our comfort also keeps us from feeling at home. It keeps us from bonding to the new culture. If we don't feel at home developing a sense of belonging, we will not be apt to stay very long.

I think the greatest hindrance for effectiveness in the city and the greatest force causing many to resist the urban calling is affluence. In Luke 12:15, Jesus said, "Beware, and be on your guard against every form of greed; for not even when one has an abundance does his life consist of his possessions." Anyone called to the ministry must guard himself from falling into such a cunning and divisive trap.

THE SECOND GREATEST HINDRANCE TO EFFECTIVE CHURCH PLANTING IN URBAN AREAS

If the greatest hindrance to effective church planting in the cities is the culturally inbred desire for the American Dream, I think the second greatest hindrance is the lack of burden and support of churches that are trying to reach people in a very difficult urban culture. Those who flee the cities for better living conditions, thinking they're moving away from violence, drugs, and poor education, have found—or will soon find—those influences at their doorstep. The influence begins in the city and flows to the smaller towns and even to other countries. I continually hear of drug and even gang problems in small towns. These problems were non-existent ten years ago. Where did these problems come from? They were exported from the city. Not only does all the good, bad, and ugly flow out of the cities to the rest of society, but the cities also export tremendous spiritual influence. The fact of urban influence should provide much impetus for all churches worldwide to reach the cities for Christ.

Just the sheer number of people living in the cities demonstrates the need to reach them. I have been appalled by many churches outside of large cities that have no burden to reach the masses in the cities. Many church mission committees will only support "foreign missions." All churches need to emphasize the importance of supporting missionaries in large cities, funding projects for the economically starved urban church, and sending mission teams to assist these Bible-based ministries. We also need to challenge our young men and women to the task of urban evangelization and discipleship as we pray regularly for the salvation of the masses in the cities.

THE GREATEST ASSET TO EFFECTIVE CHURCH PLANTING IN URBAN AREAS

What would be the greatest asset to effective church planting? Some might say adequate funding for salary and start-up costs. Others might say choosing a fast growing and perhaps upper middle class area would be the greatest benefit. Still others might claim that a qualified team to work with you would be the greatest advantage. Though these assets may be helpful to the urban church planter, I do not believe any of them even come close to the greatest and most dynamic asset that will launch you into a blessed ministry.

Other than the power of God and the Word of God, I believe your greatest asset is becoming a man or woman of faith. Hebrews 11:6 says, "And without faith it is impossible to please him." God desires each of his ministers to trust him and to live out that faith day in and day out.

My son, who is planting a church in the inner city of Chicago, went to his rented school building for his Sunday services only to have his portable sound equipment stolen out of the van. He had launched his Sunday services only a few weeks earlier. What a discouragement this was to many in his small fellowship. My son was able to remind them that there was no need for discouragement; God is in charge and would provide their needs. On a speaking engagement the following week, he shared the story of how $1,800 of new equipment had been stolen from his infant church. A man in the audience was prompted to write a check for the total amount. With this donation they were able to purchase replacement equipment before the following Sunday. They didn't miss one service before God provided.

The urban church planter will face many challenges and discouragements as he labors to grow his church. Satan will attempt to discourage the leaders as well as the lay people. How will he respond? Will he trust God who is able to take care of him and his church? If he will live by faith before his people, God will bless many times over with his abundant provision. The lessons learned will be many, and the growth experience will be irreplaceable.

Many who plant churches in the city will have to raise missionary support to fund their salaries. Where will the money come from? I have watched men who had absolutely no potential support base see God provide the money they needed from totally unexpected sources. Ephesians 3:20 says, "Now to him who is able to do far more abundantly beyond all that we ask or think, according to the power that works within us." Not only is God able, he delights in providing when we exercise faith. God wants to show his people how great and magnificent he really is. But the leaders must live by faith.

What is biblical faith, and how can I become a man or woman of faith? Many have mistakenly defined faith, thinking it had to do with a feeling or some sort of spiritual gift. There is a spiritual gift of faith but that's not what I am referring to. The faith I am talking about is faith we are all commanded to have. Faith is not a feeling. A feeling may be experienced as a by-product but we must not look for a feeling to determine if we have faith. Faith is simply a decision to take God at his word and act on it. When God promises to provide, protect, or lead, we take him at his word and make a decision of faith. Faith always requires action.

Look at Hebrews 11 and you will see that each of the characters in this great Faith's Hall of Fame believed God and acted on their faith. For example, Noah believed God and built an ark. God had told him there would be a flood, even though it had never rained to that point in the history of the earth. Even though it didn't make human sense and Noah risked ridicule, he made a decision and spent 120 years building an ark. Another example is Abraham. God had promised him that he would bless his family, multiplying his descendants to as many as the stars in the heavens. When God told Abraham to take his only son Isaac up the mountain and offer him as a sacrifice, Abraham did not hesitate. In fact, he got up early the next morning. Abraham knew that either God would stop him from killing his son or he would raise him from the dead (Heb 11:19), even though there had never been a resurrection in recorded biblical history to that date. Abraham believed God and made a decision of faith. He acted on his faith and got up early to do what God had commanded.

Let's look at one more passage. Do you ever worry? Are you anxious at times? Philippians 4:6 says, "Be anxious for nothing, but in everything by prayer and supplication with thanksgiving let your requests be made known to God." Worry is the opposite of faith. God commands us not to worry or be anxious but instead tells us we are to pray. How do we know God will help us? At the end of the previous verse the Apostle Paul tells us that "the Lord is near" (v. 5). Our decision of faith is to trust God and to stop worrying and to pray for the need or problem we are anxious about. If we obey these two commands, God promises to give us peace. Verse 7 says, "And the peace of God, which surpasses all comprehension, will guard your hearts and your minds in Christ Jesus." A number of years ago when my three youngest children were teenagers, they were out extra late at a church function. As I lay in bed wondering why they were so late, I made a decision of faith. I told the Lord I would not worry but asked if he would please bring my kids home safely. As I said the word "safely," almost between syllables, the door opened, and they were home. The next night they were in the final night of the special youth week, coming home even later than the night before. I once again made a decision of faith. I chose not to worry and asked God to please bring them home safely. Once again, right as I said the word "safely," the door opened, and they were home.

Unfortunately, most people that pray for God's help or provision begin thinking about the "what ifs" before God has a chance to answer. They think of everything that could happen and Satan robs them of the peace God just gave them. This wouldn't happen if we would only follow the next verses, Philippians 4:8–9, which says, "Finally, brethren, whatever is true, whatever is honorable, whatever is right, whatever is pure, whatever is lovely, whatever is of good repute, if there is any excellence and if anything worthy of praise, dwell on these things. The things you have learned and received and heard and seen in me, practice these things, and the God of peace will be with you." We should not allow the worry and anxiety to creep in all over again. We should meditate on the good things listed in these verses, putting our trust in God.

As we read God's Word, we must always believe everything he tells us and respond to the instruction by active faith. As we do, God will keep his word and we will grow as men and women of faith. God wants to grow our faith. He will do great things in and through us if we will but trust him. God wants to bless the church plants that model faith before the people. Being a man or woman of faith is the greatest asset a church planter can ever have.

REVIEW QUESTIONS

1. What three conditions should be met before we begin selecting a team to reach people in an urban setting and what criteria should be looked for in the team selection process?
2. What steps does the author recommend for planting an urban church?
3. What reasons does the author state is preventing so many from moving to the cities and serving in urban ministry?
4. What is the second greatest hindrance to effective church planting in urban areas?
5. What is the greatest asset of effective church planting?

Appendix

Test Yourself: The Burnout Checklist

(Note: This focuses only on burnout;
it is not a questionnaire on stress in general.)

REVIEW THE PAST TWELVE months of your *total* life—work, social situations, family, and recreation. Reflect on each of the following questions and rate the amount of change that has occurred during this period. More emphasis should be placed on change that has occurred during the past 6 months.

Use the following scale and assign a number in the rating column that reflects the degree of change you have experienced. *Be honest.* The value of this self-assessment is negligible if you are not.

1 No, or little change	2 Just noticeable change	3 Noticeable change	4 Fair degree of change	5 Great degree of change

RATING

1._____ Do you become more fatigued, tired, or worn out by the end of the day?

2._____ Have you lost interest in your present work?

3._____ Have you lost ambition in your overall career?

4._____ Do you find yourself becoming easily bored (spending long hours with nothing significant to do)?

5._____ Do you find that you have become more pessimistic, critical, or cynical of yourself or others?

6._____ Do you forget appointments, deadlines, or activities, and do not feel concerned about it?

7._____ Do you spend more time alone, withdrawn from friends, family, and work acquaintances?

8._____ Has any increase occurred in your general level of irritability, hostility, or aggressiveness?

9._____ Has your sense of humor become less obvious to yourself or others?

10._____ Do you become sick more easily (flu, colds, or problems with pain)?

11._____ Do you experience headaches more than usual?

12._____ Do you suffer from gastrointestinal problems (stomach pains, chronic diarrhea, or colitis)?

13._____ Do you wake up feeling extremely tired and exhausted most mornings?

14._____ Do you find that you deliberately try to avoid people you previously did not mind being around?

15._____ Has there been a lessening of your sexual drive?

16._____ Do you find that you now tend to treat people as impersonal objects or with a fair degree of callousness?

17._____ Do you feel you are not accomplishing anything worthwhile in your work and that you are ineffective in making any changes?

18._____ Do you feel you are not accomplishing anything worthwhile in your personal life or you have lost spontaneity in your activities?

19._____ Do you spend much time each day thinking or worrying about your job or people, future, or past?

20._____ Are you at the end of your tether, the point of breaking down or cracking up?

_____ Total Score

INTERPRETATION

Please remember, no inventory is absolutely accurate or foolproof. Your score on this Burnout Checklist is merely a guide to your experience of burnout. Take it as an indication that your life may be out of control. If your score is high, take steps toward finding help by consulting your family physician, psychotherapist, spiritual counselor, or personal advisor. The first step toward relief from burnout is to acknowledge, without being self-rejecting, that you have a problem.

20–30	There is no burnout. You may be taking your life or work too casually.
31–45	This is a normal score for anyone who works hard and seriously. Relax periodically.
46–60	This is a normal score for anyone who works hard and seriously. Relax periodically.
61–75	You are beginning to experience burnout. Take steps to better control your life.
76–90	You are burning out. You should seek help, reevaluate your present life, and make changes.
90 or higher	You are dangerously burned out and need immediate relief. Your burnout is threatening your physical and mental well-being.

Provided by Dr. Archibald Hart, Arcadia, California.
Used by permission.
Enrichment Journal
1445 Boonville Ave., Springfield, MO 65802
Email: enrichmentjournal@ag.org
Phone: (417) 862-2781, ext. 4095

Bibliography

Adair, James. *A New Look at the Old Lighthouse*. Chicago: PGM, 1996.

Adsit, Christopher B. *Personal Disciplemaking*. Orlando: Campus Crusade for Christ, 1996.

Allen, Michael N. "New Wineskin—Same Vintage Wine: Five Paths of Effective Urban Evangelism." In *A Heart for the City*, edited by John Fuder. Chicago: Moody, 1999.

American Foundation for Suicide Prevention. "Facts and Figures" (2007). Online: http://www.afsp.org/index.cfm?fuseaction=home.viewpage&page_id=050fea9f-b064-4092-b1135c3a70de1fda.

Bakke, Ray. *A Biblical Word for an Urban World*. Valley Forge, PA: The Board of International Ministries, American Baptist Church in the U.S.A., 2000.

———. *A Theology as Big as the City*. Downers Grove: InterVarsity, 1997.

———. "Foreword." In *A Heart for the City*, edited by John Fuder. Chicago: Moody, 1999.

Barna, George. *A Profile of Protestant Pastors*. The Barna Group, 2001. Online: http://barna.org/barna-update/article/5-barna-update/59-a-profile-of-protestant-pastors-in-anticipation-of-qpastor-appreciation-monthq?q=2001.

———. *Growing True Disciples*. Colorado Springs: Waterbrook, 2001.

———. *Pastor Paid Better but Attendance Unchanged*. The Barna Group, 2001. Online: http://www.barna.org/barna-update/article/5-barna-update/39-pastor-paid-better-but-attendance-unchanged.

Barnes, Albert. *Barnes' Notes on the New Testament*. Cedar Rapids, IA: Parsons Technology, 1999.

Beadle, Muriel. *A Child's Mind*. London: MacGibbon & Kee, 1971.

Benjamin, Walter W. "Fatherless Heaven, Fatherless Children." *The Wall Street Journal*, August 16, 1995.

Biehl, Bobb MacGregor, and Jerry Glen Urquhart. *Mentoring: How To Find A Mentor And How To Become One*. Masterplanning Group International, Poulsbo, WA, 1994.

Brown, David C., and Dana Thomas. "Ministering in the Projects." In *A Heart for the City*, edited by John Fuder. Chicago: Moody, 1999.

Brown, Francis. *The New Hebrew and English Lexicon*. Peabody, MA: Hendrickson, 1979.

Buddin, Sharon. National Association of Secondary Schools Principles. "Report on the State of High Schools." Keynote address, 2002.

Cairns, Earle E. *Christianity Through the Centuries, A History of the Christian Church*. Grand Rapids: Zondervan, 1996.

Carroll, Lewis. *The Adventures of Alice in Wonderland*, edited by John Berseth. Mineola, NY: Dover, 2001.

Claerbaut, David. *Urban Ministry in a New Millennium*. Federal Way, WA: World Vision, 2005.

Coleman, Robert E. *The Master Plan of Discipleship*. Grand Rapids: Revel, Spire Edition, 1998.

———. *The Master Plan of Evangelism*. Grand Rapids: Revel, 1993.

Commission on Children at Risk, The. *Hardwired to Connect: The Scientific Case for Authoritative Communities*. New York: Institute for American, 1996.

Dahmer, Lionel. *A Father's Story*. New York: William Morrow, 1994.

Gage, Warren. *The Ethiopian Eunuch Finds Joy*. Knox Theological Seminary, Fort Lauderdale. Online: http://knoxseminary.org/Prospective/Faculty/KnoxPulpit/wgage_eunuch.html.

Gallup, George H. "Vital Signs." *Leadership*, Fall 1987.

Garriott, Maria. "Priscilla's Progeny: American Women in Urban Ministry." In *Urban Mission*, September 1996.

Greenway, Roger. *Apostles to the City*. Grand Rapids: Baker, 1978.

Greenway, Roger, and Timothy M. Monsma. *Cities: Missions' New Frontier*. Grand Rapids: Baker, 1994.

Grigg, Viv. *Companion to the Poor.* Monrovia: MARC, 1990.

Hadidian, Allen. *Successful Discipling*. Chicago: Moody, 1979.

Hart, Archibald D. "Burnout: Prevention and Cure." Helpguide.org, 2008. Full list of symptoms online: http://www.churchlink.com.au:80/churchlink/forum/r_croucher/stress_burnout.html. Condensed list online: http://helpguide.org/mental/burnout_signs_symptoms.htm.

Henrichsen, Walter. *Disciples are Made Not Born*. Colorado Springs: Cook Communications, 1988.

Hill, A. Anne, and June O'Neill. "Underclass Behaviors in the United States." CUNY, Baruch College. Illinois Department of Public Health, 1993.

Home School Legal Defense Association. Purcellville, VA: Online: http://www.hslda.org.

Hudson, Winthrop S. *The Great Tradition of the American Churches*. New York: Harper & Roe, 1953.

Jackson, Thomas. *Centenary of Wesleyan Methodism*. New York: T. Mason & G. Lane, 1839.

Kane, J. Herbert. *A Global View of Christian Missions*. Grand Rapids: Baker, 2009.

Latourette, Kenneth Scott. *A History of Christianity.* New York: Harper and Row, 1953.

Lazere, Edward. *In Short Supply: The Growing Affordable Housing Gap.* Center on Budget and Policy Priorities. Washington, DC, 1995.

Lewis, Robert. *Men's Fraternity: Quest for Authentic Manhood, session 6*, "Remembering Dad." LifeWay Press, 2004. Online: http://www.mensfraternity.com/shop/default.aspx.

———. *Men's Fraternity: Quest for Authentic Manhood, session 23*, "Fathers and Daughters." LifeWay Press, 2004. Online: http://www.mensfraternity.com/shop/default.aspx.

Linthicum, Robert C. "Networking, Hope for the City." In *Planting and Growing Urban Churches: From Dream to Reality*, edited by Harvie M. Conn. Grand Rapids: Baker, 1999.

Locke, Tom. "Reaching Youth Involved in Gangs." In *A Heart for the City*, edited by John Fuder. Chicago: Moody, 1999.

Lockyer, Herbert. *All the Promises of the Bible*. Grand Rapids: Zondervan, 1962.

Marciniak, Ed. (Orientation Address, Seminary Consortium for Urban Pastoral Education Orientation.) Chicago: Latino Seminario, September 23, 1978; *Reviving an Inner City Community*. (Chicago: Center for Research in Urban Government, 1977.)

Mead, Connie. "Kids With Kids, New Moms Cares for Unwed Teenage Mothers and their Children." In *A Heart for the City*, edited by John Fuder. Chicago: Moody, 1999. Extrapolated from The Illinois Department of Public Health, online: http://www.idph.state.il.us/health/statshome.htm#Total.

Merriam-Webster's Collegiate Dictionary Tenth Edition. Springfield: Merriam-Webster, Incorporated, 1998.

Moore, Waylon B. *New Testament Follow-up*. Grand Rapids: Eerdmans, 1963.

Morehouse Conference on African American Fathers. *Turning the Corner on Father Absence in Black America*. Atlanta: Morehouse Research Institute, 1999.

Morgan, G. Campbell. *Preaching*. London: Oliphants, 1967.

Morrison, James L. University of North Carolina, Chapel Hill, NC, lecture. Online: http://horizon.unc.edu/projects/presentations/Wfs/sld035.html. Nashville: LifeWay, 2004. Online: http://www.mensfraternity.com/Shop/Default.aspx.

Myers, Bryant. *The Changing Shape of World Missions*. Monrovia: MARC, 1993.

National Center for Fathering. "The Extent of Fatherlessness." Gallup Youth Survey 4, June, 1997. Online: http://www.fathers.com/content/index.php?option=com_content&task=view&id=336.

National Institute on Alcohol Abuse and Alcoholism. *Children of Alcoholics: Are they Different?* US Department of Health and Human Services, 1990. Online: http://pubs.niaaa.nih.gov/publications/aa09.htm.

Nowak, Mark W. "Immigration and U.S. Population Growth: An Environmental Prospective." *NPG Special Report*. Online: http://www.npg.org/specialreports/immxuspopgrowth.htm.

OAS Report. *Suicide Thoughts, Suicide Attempts, Major Depressive Episodes, and Substance Use among Adults*. Office of Applied Studies, Substance Abuse and Mental Health Services Administration, December, 2008.

PBS Health Spotlight. "The Evolution of Nursing Home Care in the United States." Online: http://www.pbs.org/newshour/health/nursinghomes/timeline.html.

Population Division of the Department of Economic and Social Affairs of the United Nations Secretariat. "World Population Prospectus: The 1999 Revision." Online: http://www.un.org/esa/population/publications/wup1999/urbanization.pdf.

———. "World Population Prospectus: The 2003 Revision." Online: http://www.un.org/esa/population/publications/wup2003/WUP2003Report.pdf.

———. "World Urbanization Prospectus: The 2005 Revision." Online: http://www.un.org/esa/population/publications/WUP2005/2005wup.htm.

Redeemer. *The Importance of the City*. Manhattan, NY: Redeemer Presbyterian Church. n.d.

Schaff, Philip. *History of the Christian Church*. Vol. 1. Peabody, MA: Hendrickson, 1985.

Schiffman, Betsy. "Home Improvement: Most Overpriced Places 2004." *Forbes Magazine*. Online: http://www.forbes.com/lists/2004/08/13/cx_bs_0813home.html.

Sims, W. H. *Baptist Hymnal*, 272.

Singer, Audrey. "The New Metropolitan Geography of U.S. Immigration." Washington D.C: Brookings Institute, Center on Urban and Metropolitan Policy, Feb. 2006. Online: http://www.brookings.edu/urban.

———. "The Rise of New Immigrant Gateways." Washington D.C: Brookings Institute, Center on Urban and Metropolitan Policy. Online: www.brookings.edu/urban.

Sjögren, Steve. "Servant Evangelism: Kindness Campaigns." In *Loving Your City Into the Kingdom*, edited by Ted Haggard and Jack Hayford. Ventura, CA: Regal, 1997.

Smith, Douglas A., and G. Roger Jarjoura. "Social Structure and Criminal Victimization." Journal of Research in Crime and Delinquency; epitomizing in The Family in America: New Research, June 1988. Cited in Amneus, The Garbage Generation.

Stark, Rodney. *Cities of God*. New York: HarperCollins, 2006.

United Nations Population Fund. "World Population 2009. Facing a Changing World: Women, Population and Climate." Online: http://www.unfpa.org/swp/2009/en/pdf/EN_SOWP09.pdf.

U.S. Census Bureau. "Annual Social and Economic." Online: http://pubdb3.census.gov/macro/032008/pov/toc.htm, Supplement. 2008.

———. "Urban and Rural Classification." 2000. Online: www.census.gov/geo/www/ua/ua_2k.html.

U.S. Department of Justice, Office of Justice Programs National Institute of Justice. "What Can the Federal Government Do To Decrease Crime and Revitalize Communities?" January 5–7, 1998. Online: http://www.ncjrs.gov/pdffiles/172210.pdf.

Walvoord, John F., and Roy B Zuck. *The Bible Knowledge Commentary: An Exposition of the Scriptures by Dallas Seminary Faculty*. Wheaton, IL: Victor Books, 1985.

Wikipeda. "Demographics of the United States." August 2010. Online: http://en.wikipedia.org/wiki/Demographics_of_the_United_States.

Wilkin, Michael. *Following The Master: A Biblical Theology of Discipleship*. Grand Rapids: Zondervan, 1992.

Yamamori, Tetsunao. "How to Reach Urban Ethnics." Urban Mission Newsletter, March, 1984. Philadelphia: Westminster Theological Seminary.